VEGAN MEAL PREP COOKBOOK FOR ATHLETES

2 Books in 1:
Ready-to-Go and High-Protein Meals
with 120+ Delicious Vegan Recipes

Mark Power

TABLE OF CONTENTS

VEGAN MEAL PREP FOR BEGINNERS

Ready-to-Go Meals for Weight Loss and Healthy Eating. An Easy Guide with 4 Weekly Plans and Vegan Recipes

Congratulations on purchasing *Vegan Meal Prep for Beginners.*

The following chapters will discuss everything you need to know to get started with the vegan diet and add in some of the meal prep parts that we need. There are so many things out there to enjoy when it comes to following the vegan diet, and it is one of the best dietary choices to go with when you want to lose weight and improve your health. But it is sometimes hard to stick with it and be prepared. And that is why we will introduce meal planning into this and learn how to combine the vegan diet with meal planning tips to make life easier.

At the beginning of this diet plan will take a look at the vegan diet and what it is. We will start with some of the many health benefits of this diet plan and why so many people want to jump on and learn more about following it easily. We can then learn more about the foods that are allowed and the ones that you should avoid to get results with this diet plan.

Once we know a bit more about the vegan diet and what it is all about, it is time for us to jump in and learn more about meal prepping. We are going to take a look at what meal prepping is and some of the benefits of using this, how to prepare your kitchen so it is ready for some of the meal prep, and the vegan diet in general. Then we will talk about how you can find the best meals and recipes for your needs when it comes to the vegan diet so you can enjoy your meal plan as well.

From there, it is time to take a look at some of the other exciting things that we can do when it comes to preparing for the vegan diet with some meal planning. We will look at how meal prepping can help you lose weight and reach all of your health goals, how to organize your shopping list, and some of the basics of the meal plan to help you get started, including four weeks of meal prep ideas to help you get going on this plan.

At the end of this guidebook, you will take a look at the recipes you can use when it comes to working on this kind of diet plan. There are so many delicious vegan recipes that you can work with. We will take a look at those that work for breakfast, lunch, dinner, and dessert so that you can make some of the best recipes for your needs and ensure that you are able to really get healthy and ready to handle your meal planning goals in no time.

There are many benefits of the vegan diet, and when you combine it with some of the benefits that come with the meal planning that we will talk about in this guidebook, you are sure to see a lot of results in the process. It is a fast and easy way to make sure that you are getting all of your nutrients and can make weight loss and good health fall into your grasp faster than ever before. When you are ready to get started with how to use meal planning to follow the vegan diet, check out this guidebook to help.

Last but not least important, avoiding animal products is one of the most obvious ways you can take a stand against animal cruelty and animal exploitation everywhere.

There are plenty of books on this subject on the market, thanks again for choosing this one! Every effort was made to ensure it is full of as much useful information as possible; please enjoy it!

PART 1

ALL ABOUT THE VEGAN DIET

Chapter 1 - The Many Benefits of the Vegan Diet

There are a lot of diet plans out there that we can choose to follow. Some will be low fat and encourage us to eat lots of healthy carbs and fruits and vegetables. Some will be low carb and will take it the completely other way and have you cut out the carbs and ramp up the number of fats you eat. Then there are more about getting lots of protein into your day, which can be a great option. Then, some diets are more about just having moderation on all of the foods you eat and don't lean too much one way or another.

But the diet plan that we are going to discuss in this guidebook is known as the vegan diet. This is a healthy diet that is good for helping people to lose weight and provides us with a ton of other health benefits in the process as well. It can help us maintain a healthy heart, fight against certain types of cancers, and fight against type two diabetes.

Basically, the vegan diet is all about cutting out all animal sources of food and any animal products. This means that things like meat out are not only things, but eggs and many types of dairy are going to be restricted as well. Many people go on this diet because it helps them eliminate some of the bad things in their lives and make it easier to lose weight and improve their health. But many people like to go on this kind of diet because of ethical reasons or because they want to keep things better for the environment.

There are many benefits that you can enjoy when it comes to a vegan diet and following it for your health. Some of the best benefits that you can enjoy when it comes to the vegan diet will include:

It Is Rich in Nutrients

If you switch from the typical American diet over to a vegan diet, you are indeed going to eliminate a lot of animal and meat products. This is going to lead you to rely more on some of the other foods out there. If you are working with the whole-foods version of the vegan diet, the replacements you will work with will take whole grains, nuts and seeds, peas, beans, fruits, and vegetables. Since these foods are going to really take up a big proportion of the vegan diet compared to what we see in the typical American diet, they are going to ensure that we take in a higher amount of some of the beneficial nutrients that our body needs.

For example, several studies have shown that these kinds of diets are going to provide the body with more antioxidants and more fiber than the traditional diet. They will also be higher in things like vitamins A, C, and E, along with folate, magnesium, and potassium, all of which are good for us. We have to keep in mind, though, that not all of the vegan diet versions are going to be equal. For example, some of the vegan diets out there will not be well-planned and will not provide us with the right amounts of essential fatty acids, zinc, iodine, calcium, iron, or vitamin B12. This is why it is important to stay away from the fast-food or nutrient-poor options for the vegan diet. They may be considered vegan, but this does not mean that they are good for you. You should base the diet around whole and nutrient-rich plants and fortified foods. You can even consider starting with a supplement like a vitamin B12 to help at the beginning of this diet.

Helps Get Rid of Extra Weight

Many people are deciding to turn to a diet based on plants to help them get rid of their extra weight, and there is a lot of good reason for that. Several observational studies show how most vegans, at least the ones who follow the diet properly, will be thinner and have a lower body mass index than those who are not vegans. Also, a few randomized controlled studies can report that these vegan diets will be more effective for weight loss than any of the diets compared to them.

One of these studies showed that the vegan diet helped those who followed it lose 9.3 pounds more than those in a control diet of another sort over an 18-week study period. Interestingly, the ones who followed the vegan diet lost more weight than those who had to follow the calorie-restricted diets, even though the vegan groups did not count calories and were allowed to eat until they felt full.

What is more with this is that in a study that compared the weight loss effects that show up in five different diets, it was found that both the vegetarian and the vegan diets were just as well-accepted as some of the results in the standard Western diets and the semi-vegetarian diets. Even when they were not following these diets 100 percent, the vegan and the vegetarian groups were still able to lose more weight than those who went on one of the standard Western diets as well.

Helps to Lower Blood Sugar Levels

Going vegan could help out those who are suffering from type 2 diabetes and declining kidney function. Vegans are going to have lower levels of blood sugars, a higher sensitivity to insulin, and their risk of developing type 2 diabetes in the first place can go down by up to 78 percent. Studies even show that the vegan diet can lower the levels of blood sugars in those who are diabetic more than some of the best-known diets out there, even compared to the diet recommended by the American Diabetes Association.

In one study that was done on this, about 43 percent of the participants who were following a vegan diet were able to reduce their dosage of medications that they used to lower blood sugars. In contrast, only 26 percent of those on a diet recommended by the ADA were able to do the same. Some other studies report that people with diabetes who substitute meat for plant protein may be able to reduce their risk of poor kidney functioning as well.

If you are someone who is dealing with higher levels of blood sugars, then the vegan diet is going to be the right one for you to use as well. It is simple, and it is one of the best ways to get your blood sugar levels down and to a more manageable amount in no time.

May Be Able To Protect Against Cancers

According to the World Health Organization, about one-third of all cancers can be prevented by factors within our control, and one of these is the diet that we follow. For example, eating legumes on a regular basis may be enough to help reduce our risk of colorectal cancer by up to 18 percent. Research also suggests that eating at least seven portions of fresh fruits and vegetables per day may help to lower our risk of dying from cancer up to 15 percent.

As we can imagine, vegans are generally going to eat more legumes, fruits, and vegetables compared to those who do not follow this kind of eating plan. This could explain why a recent review that went over 96 studies found that vegans can have a 15 percent lower risk of developing or dying from cancer. What's more, vegan diets are going to contain more soy products, which are believed to offer some protection against breast cancer.

Avoiding some of the animal products found in the traditional diet could be what will help reduce the risk of colon cancers, breast cancers, and even prostate cancers. This could be due to the fact that vegan diets are going to be without smoked or processed meats or other types of meats that are cooked at high temperatures. Which could promote some types of cancers? Vegans are also going to avoid a lot of dairy products, which are thought to increase the risk of prostate cancer.

Lowers Your Risk of Heart Disease

Eating fresh fruits, vegetables, legumes, and fiber is going to be linked to a lower risk of heart disease overall. All of these are going to be eaten in a relatively large amount when we are on a vegan diet that has been planned out well. Observational studies that compare vegans and the general public found that those who were vegan had about a 75 percent lower risk of developing high blood pressure at some point. Vegans could also have up to a 42 percent lower risk of dying of heart disease as well.

In addition to all of this, there are more randomized and controlled studies out there that show us how the vegan diet is going to be more effective when it comes to reducing LDL cholesterol, reducing blood sugar levels, and even the total cholesterol levels of those who follow them compared to any of the other diets we look at. This can be really beneficial to the health of the heart since reducing all three of these things can reduce your risk of developing heart disease at some point by up to 46 percent.

Can Reduce Arthritis Pain

There are even a few studies out there that have taken a look at how the vegan diet has such a positive effect on people who suffer from various forms of arthritis in their lives. One study randomly took 40 arthritis participants and had them either continue to follow their traditional omnivorous diet or switched some of them to a plant-based and whole-food vegan diet. Both had to follow it for six weeks total.

Those who went on the vegan diet reported that they had higher energy levels and better general functioning than those who didn't make any changes to their diet. Two other studies then took the time to investigate the effects of a probiotic-rich, raw food vegan diet on rheumatoid arthritis symptoms. Both of these reported that those who went in the vegan group experienced much better improvements in many symptoms, including morning stiffness, joint swelling, and pain compared to those on a traditional kind of diet.

As we can see, there are a lot of benefits that come with following this kind of diet plan, and pretty much anyone is able to benefit from using it for their own needs. With the right types of foods, and making sure that we don't fall into the trap of assuming that just because it says it is vegan doesn't mean it is a good option to eat, we will be able to eat a much healthier lifestyle that is good for us.

How Do I Follow the Vegan Diet?

Now that we have had a chance to take a look at some of the benefits that we need to work with when it comes to choosing the vegan diet, it is now time to take a look at some of the steps that we can take in order to stick with this diet. We already know some of the basics, such as those on this diet are not allowed to eat meats, but we have to remember that animal products, or anything that comes from an animal, like milk and eggs, had to be avoided as well.

We will take a look at some of the foods that you can eat on this kind of diet plan first. There are a lot of great tasting foods that you are going to love and can really spice up your meals, though it may seem like you are limited when you first get started. Some of the different foods that you are able to consume when you are on the vegan diet will include:

1. *Legumes:* This would include lots of different foods like lentils, beans, and peas. These are going to provide us with a lot of beneficial compounds from plants and other nutrients that can keep us nice and healthy as long as we need it.

2. *Nuts and nut kinds of butter:* You will find that the unroasted and unblanched versions are going to be the best. You should also stay away from those that are

salted or have extra things on them, that means don't go out and buy the candied ones or the ones covered in chocolate and assume you are getting all of the good benefits.

3. ***Tempeh, seitan, and tofu:*** These are some of the best options to go with when it comes to finding lots of protein on this diet. Since you have to kick out eggs, fish, meat, and poultry on this one, you will find that adding in the three options above can be a good choice to get your protein and other nutrients still.

4. ***Seeds:*** these do have some of the protein and the omega-3 fatty acids that are hard to get on this diet plan, along with some of the other nutrients that your body may be needed at the time. You will want to stick with some of the options like flaxseeds, chia, and hemp to get the most benefits.

5. ***Nutritional yeast:*** This is another way to add in a bit more protein to any of the vegan dishes you work with. And it can kind of add in a cheese flavor to these dishes as well. If you are able to find a variety that is fortified with B12, then go with this option as well.

6. ***Plant yogurts and milk that are fortified with calcium can be good options as well:*** these are going to ensure that you can get in all of the calcium that you need. And there are a lot of different varieties, so you are sure to find the one that works the best for your needs.

7. ***Fruits and vegetables:*** are both going to be awesome foods to go with to increase your intake of nutrients. You can go with many different types of these to keep yourself healthy and provide more of the nutrients that our bodies need to be strong and do well.

8. ***Whole grains and cereals.*** These will be good sources of some of the minerals that we need, along with the B-vitamins, iron, fiber, and the complex carbs that we need to make it through the day. Many options come with this one; you just need to take the time to pick out the

wholesome ones, not the baked goods or other processed pieces of bread, to keep yourself healthy on this diet plan.

Now that we know a bit more about the foods that we are allowed to have on the vegan diet, it is time to look at some of the foods we should avoid instead. Vegans are going to make it their goal to avoid eating any animal foods, and they will need to avoid foods that contain ingredients that come from an animal as well. This is going to limit a few of the foods that you may be used to enjoying on a traditional diet. But these are taken away to help improve your health, along with a few other reasons as well. Some of the foods that we need to avoid when it comes to following the vegan diet includes:

1. ***Poultry and meat:*** This is going to include any of the meat sources that you may have had in the past. The obvious choices like beef, organ meat, chicken, goose, turkey, and more all need to be taken off. If it comes from an animal, you are not supposed to eat it on this diet plan.

2. ***Animal-based ingredients:*** These are a bit harder to work with or recognize, but they are based on animals and those products, so they are essential to kick out as well. You will want to avoid things like shellac, gelatin, albumen from egg whites, lactose, whey, and casein, for example.

3. ***Fish and seafood:*** These are going to fit into the category of meat products as well, so anything that you are able to catch and eat from the sea, you will need to avoid when you go on this kind of diet plan as well.

4. ***Bee products:*** Any of the products that come from bees needs to be avoided when you are on this kind of diet as well. This means that things like the royal jelly, bee pollen, and honey all need to be taken from the list as well.

5. ***Dairy:*** This is going to include lots of different options that we may be used to having on this kind of diet. Of course, it means that we need to avoid the milk

and cheeses, though there are some vegan alternatives that you can choose to enjoy, and we also need to avoid options like ice cream, butter, yogurt, and cream.

6. ***Eggs:*** And finally, we need to be careful about eggs as well. There are ways to make your own eggs in this kind of diet plan, but you should not eat the traditional eggs or not follow this diet plan. Any eggs that come from options like fish, chickens, quails, or ostriches should be avoided.

Following the vegan diet will be a little bit different from what we may be used to working with in the past and with our traditional diets, but it is one of the best choices you can make for your overall health and well-being well. If you are worried about following this kind of plan, we will go through and talk about some of the meal prepping things that you can do to make it easier as we go through this guidebook. This will ensure that you are able to really get in control over the process and that you will not feel like you are drowning or not able to keep up as you go through this process.

CHAPTER 2 - ALL ABOUT MEAL PREPPING

Now it is time for us to dive into some of the basics that come with meal prepping and why this is going to be the best thing for you when you first get started on the vegan diet. When you were reading through some of the different rules and guidelines of the vegan diet, it may have seemed a bit overwhelming at first. But when we are able to add in a little bit of meal planning to the mix, it makes it a whole lot easier. We won't have to struggle each night to throw things together and worry about what recipes we will create and use. We can instead focus on doing this all at once and just take the rest of the week off to relax. With that in mind, let's dive into some of the basics of meal prepping and how it can be so good for the vegan diet.

The Different Ways to Meal Prep

Many people assume that there is only one way they can meal prep, and if that method doesn't work for them, then there is no point in even trying at all. They don't realize that there are quite a few ways to work on meal prepping, and we will take some time to look at some of the methods that we can use. Some of the most popular methods of meal prepping that are out there that you can choose will include:

1. The meals that are made ahead of time. These are going to be when we cook up full meals ahead of time, and then we put them in the freezer or fridge. Then, when it is time to use them, we just have to heat them back up. This can be really helpful when it comes to dinner when everyone is tired and hungry. You can put one in the oven and then cook it up without doing all of the other steps.

2. Batch cooking. This is when you will make a large batch of a specific recipe and then split it into smaller portions to be frozen and eaten over the next few months. You may make a really big lasagna, and then split it into three or four and have them ready when it works for you.

3. Meals that are individually portioned. Preparing fresh meals and then portioning them into some individual grab and go portions to be put in the fridge and then eaten over a few days is another option. This can be helpful to keep you on track when you are getting some lunches ready to go for your needs.

4. Ready to cook ingredients: This is when you prepare all of the components that you need for a specific number of meals ahead of time. You will still cook the meals along the way, but the ingredients will be ready, so you can just throw them all together when it is time and get it done quickly.

The method that will work the best for you is going to depend on your own daily routine and your overall goals. If you are trying to make your morning a bit easier, for example, then preparing some breakfasts ahead of time may be the best way to help out. But some families like to have batch cooked meals in the freezer, so they are all set to go when they are limited on time in the evenings. It is possible to do some mixing and matching when it comes to doing any of the meal prepping options above, so you are able to choose the one that will work the best for you.

Picking the Right Variety of Meals

The next thing that we need to consider is how to pick out the right variety of meals. Figuring out how many meals to make and what you would like to include in each of the meals is going to be tricky. The best way to plan for this is to decide which meals would be the best to focus on and which meal is prepping methods seems to be the best. Then you can check out your calendar to see how many of each meal you would like to prepare ahead of time for the upcoming week. We also need to remember to account for some situations where we may go out to eat for dates, client dinners, or just hanging out with friends.

When we select which meals to make, it is best to start with a limited number of recipes that we already know. This is going to ease our transition into meal planning. We need to try not to pick out just one recipe for the whole week. This may sound like a nice idea and like it will make life easier, but in reality, it is going to lead to boredom and will lack some of the nutrients that your body needs. It can also make it so that you are less likely to stick with the meal plan.

Each person is going to be a bit different from what they would like to do here. Some will like to pick a large variety of meals and will constantly switch them out, and others are happy with sticking to a few of the same meals to keep it simple and because they know what they like. Both of these are going to work well when you handle meal planning; you just need to know which one you want to use and which one is the right choice for your needs. Don't sell yourself short on meals, though, if you are someone who likes a lot of variety because this is something that we can do when working with the idea of meal planning and all that goes with it.

The Benefits of Meal Planning

Now we need to take a look at some of the best reasons and benefits as to why we would want to work with meal planning in the first place. Isn't it just fine to make the meals as you go and not have to worry about being organized and have it all together? There are a lot of people who choose to work with regular cooking and without doing meal planning, and that is fine to go with if it is your choice. But there are a ton of benefits that come with meal planning, and we need to take a look at a few of them.

The first benefit is that it is going to take away some of the indecision. There is nothing more frustrating than opening up all of the cupboards in your kitchen to see what is there. You wait for inspiration and ideas on what to cook, but there is nothing that stands out. Indecision will waste time, and if you can't figure it out, you end up eating out and wasting money. When you have a meal plan, it is easier to go on autopilot, and you will already have all of the ingredients and even some of the meals that you need to do.

You will also find that meal planning is going to lead to fewer bad choices. When you do not have a plan for your meals, it is going to lead us to make a lot of bad choices in what we will eat. Take out, and ready meals are going to be quick and easy, and they can turn into habits if we are not that careful. And these are not healthy, even if they say they are vegan and can hit your wallet as well.

Meal planning will help remove the need to make these choices when you are tired or hungry, and when you can plan ahead of time, with a clear head, you will find that it is easier to make plans that have healthier foods with them. You can add a few treats and a few extras for fun, but you will find that overall, meal planning takes out the bad choices and helps you do a lot better.

Have you ever found yourself looking back at some of the meals and things that you have eaten, and then you realize that you have been eating something that is pretty similar each night? This is not all that bad, but when you add in some meal planning, you will find that it is easier to balance out your foods, and you can actually get more variety into some of the meals that you are eating. This can make them more exciting and ensures that it is easier to stick with the vegan diet.

There is also the benefit that this kind of prepping will help you reduce the amount of food that you waste and help you save money. If you can create your meal plans and use your food in a wise manner, you will naturally start to see a reduction in the amount of food you are wasting. Buying only what is needed for your meals, and those are the ones that you already planned out, and not being swayed by offers that have nothing to do with what you want, can help you to save a lot of money over time.

Overall, working with meal planning is going to make your life a whole lot easier. It takes a bit of work and dedication, but you will love it when you can just go to the store and only get the items you need. And it is even more fun when you are able to pull out the meal at the right time to eat, and all you have to do is heat it up without having to worry about cooking and preparing it all at that time. Get ready for the vegan diet and your weekly routine to get a lot easier.

How to Cut Down on Cooking Time

Even those who are big fans of meal prepping will not be that fond of cooking and spending hours in the kitchen to get this done. But we do need to spend at least a bit of time in the kitchen to get all of this done and make things easier during the week. Some of the steps that we are able to take to get our cooking time down as much as possible include:

1. *Stick with a consistent schedule.*
Meal prepping is going to work the best when you can still stick to a regular schedule—knowing what you are going to get at the grocery store and how to prep all of your meals will keep you in a good routine and make it easier. For example, you could choose to reserve Sunday morning to go grocery shopping and then have Monday for making lunches for the whole week. You

can choose which schedule you want to go with but pick out one and stick with it to ensure that you can get in a good groove and that you will not feel overwhelmed all of the time with it.

2. *Pick out a good combination of routines to do this with.*

Picking out the right combination of recipes is going to ensure that you are a bit more effective in the kitchen. To save time, select recipes that have different methods of cooking. If you have too many recipes that all need the same appliance, you will not be able to prepare as many recipes at a time because they will have to wait for one another. This is going to be really important when you are trying to work with some make-ahead meals or when you do any kind of batch cooking.

3. *Organize your prep and cook times.*

If you think of your workflow ahead of time, it can really make things easier in the kitchen. To help you to organize your prep and cook times, you need to start out with a recipe that will take the longest amount of time to cook. This could be something like an oven meal or soup. Once you have that meal going, move on to the rest. Reserve all of the cold meals to do last, because you can make them while the others are cooking.

You can even cut down on the cooking and prep time when you check the ingredients before you start. If you see that two or three of the recipes need diced onions, for example, you can just go through and chop out all that you need ahead of time without the worry.

4. *Make a shopping list.*

Spending time at the store can be a big waste of time. To cut down on how much time you are at the store, you can keep a detailed grocery list organized based on the supermarket departments. This is going to prevent issues with doubling back to a section that you already visited and can speed up some of the time you spend at the store. You should also try to limit the shopping to just once a week and use the grocery delivery service to help you spend fewer times hopping. This can also be a good way to cut down on your grocery bill as well.

How to be Successful with Meal Prepping

Getting a whole week's worth of meals, and sometimes more can seem like a daunting task to get started, especially when you are just beginning or trying to work with a vegan diet. The good news is that there are many ways that we can make this a bit easier. Some of the simple steps that you can follow to be successful with meal prepping includes:

1. Select the right meal prep method of choice: This can also be a combination of methods and should be based on your own nutrition goals and lifestyle.

2. Stick to a schedule: Pick one day each week that you want to do all of the meal planning, look for all of the groceries and cook.

3. Pick the right number of meals: You have to keep in mind your own personal calendar and the meals from restaurants you have planned out for the week.

4. Select the recipes that are right for you. Keep out an eye for variety and preparation methods. When you start out, it is usually best to just use some of the recipes you already know how to work with.

5. Try to find ways to reduce the time you spend on grocery shopping. Make a list that is as organized as possible or even work with shopping for your groceries online.

6. Send a little less time in the kitchen. You can choose which meals you would like to cook first and base this on the amount of time that it takes to cook those meals.

7. Store the meals. You need to work with some of the safe cooling methods and the right containers to make this happen. You can refrigerate the meals that you plan to eat within the next few days and then label and freeze all of the rest of them.

As we can see here, we are able to see a lot of benefits, and ease of use, when we are working with the idea of meal planning. It can be as simple or as complex as we would like. Some people spend a lot of o time working on meals and may get a whole month of meals up and running. And others are going to just work on a week at a time. You can customize this whole process to make it work for your needs, and it is particularly useful for sticking with the vegan diet when you are ready to get started.

CHAPTER 3 - HOW TO GET YOUR KITCHEN READY

You will quickly find that working with the vegan diet will be different from what you can see with the traditional diet that you may have been on up to this point. That is why we are going to spend a bit of time taking a look at how you can make sure that your kitchen is ready to go for this new change in your life.

As you can imagine, there will be many great fruits and vegetables that you can add to your kitchen. Keeping your fridge full of these as much as possible will be a good step in the right direction when it is time to prepare yourself for this diet. Some good spices to get the food ready and lots of healthy whole grains and legumes can be a great way to get started.

With this in mind, and outside of some of the foods that you are naturally going to add into your kitchen when you choose this diet, we are going to take a look at some of the different appliances and tools that can be so useful when you go on this diet. You can choose whether you would like to add these into the kitchen and use them as a part of this diet plan or not. It all depends on the meals that you plan to create and what your overall goals are for this. Some of the tools and appliances that you are able to use when it is time to get your kitchen ready will include:

Spiralizer

While you can make some regular noodles and follow this diet plan, if you need to add in more fruits and vegetables to get your nutrients, you may find that working with a spiralizer to prepare your plant-based noodles can be a great option to work with. You can do this with things like butternut squash or even zucchini noodles if you would like. There are a lot of these that you can go with at the grocery store.

A handheld spiralizer is not going to be that expensive to work with, but it is a bit more limited than other options. If you would like to be able to spiralize any kind of vegetable, then going with a countertop option is going to work well for this. They are a bit more in terms of cost, but they will come with a lot of the attachments that you need so that you can handle all of the noodles and more that you want to make in no time.

Cast Iron Skillet

The next option that we are going to be able to work with is a cast-iron skillet. If you take the time to treat this pan well, you may be going to have it forever. You will find that it is great for making the perfect pancakes and the expertly seared tofu. This is one of the essential tools for the home chef, whether working with the vegan diet. It is a non-stick pan without any commercial coatings that seem to be on some of the other pans you can purchase well. You will also like they are oven safe and can be like a baking dish for some of your cobblers and more if you would like to work with this.

If you are going to get a cast-iron skillet, make sure that you learn some of the rules for breaking it in and how to take care of the skillet. This will ensure that you are getting the most out of it and that it is going to work for some of your cooking needs for a long time, even when you are focusing on the vegan diet.

Air Fryer

While this appliance may not be the most compact to work with, it is going to be really helpful when you are working with a vegan diet. You will find that you can quickly make room for it when you find out how easy it can make this kind of cooking on the vegan diet. It can make light and crispy any food that you want, without any of the oil, this air-fryer is also going to help cut down on the amount of time that you have to take cooking.

You can cook pretty much anything in your new air fryer, as long as you have taken care to find a good recipe to make this happen. It is good for frying tofu, working with some of the vegetables that can often give out some trouble, and more. It is so much better than the oven and can give you some fried food taste without all of the bad stuff in it.

Blender

The higher the quality that you can get with the blender, the better it is going to be for everyone. There are many times when you will need to blend together lots of fruits and vegetables in this kind of diet, and taking the time to work with a high-quality blender will make a difference in how well that stuff turns out. There is a bit of difference between the blenders out there, and if you really want to stick with the vegan diet, then you should go with one of the better ones, like Vitamix or Blendtec, rather than saving money on one that is only $30.

This is a good investment when you are on this kind of diet plan, and picking out one that is higher in quality and will last is going to be a good thing. This is often one that you are going to work with to help make some of your sweet treats, smoothies, and sauces along the way.

Along with the same idea, you may want to consider going with a food processor. Sometimes you can work with just one of the other depending on your own needs and what you are hoping to get out of this. Go with one that will hold onto all of the foods that you need to make some of your meals. You don't want to go with one that is too big, but going with one that is a good size can make the difference in how much you are able to get done, especially if you are dealing with things like meal planning.

Steamer Basket

Another thing to consider is a steamer basket, especially one that is bamboo. You will find that unlike some of the steamer baskets that are usually offered with use in the microwave, this is going to be a great tool that will allow us to steam food in multiple layers. They are also going to be essential if you want to be able to cook some of your own buns or wantons that are homemade or if you want to work with creating some tamales.

If you are going to use one of these steamer baskets, make sure to line the bottom of this with some parchment paper. Cabbage leaves and a banana can work for this as well. Having these in place will ensure that the food will not stick at all and help it come out perfect every time.

As we can see, there are various tools that we are able to use to make cooking in the vegan diet so much easier than it would be in other situations. You can choose which option is the right one for you to use and then leave out some of the ones that you don't think you will want all that much. Sometimes, spending a few weeks working on meal planning and the vegan diet can give you a better idea of which items will be useful for you, and then you can go out and pick out the ones that you want, rather than wasting money on things and appliances that you will never use.

Chapter 4 - Healthy Meal Plan

Now it is time for us to get started on some of the basics that we can do to start on a weight loss meal prep program. If you want to see success with the vegan diet, one of the best things you can do is sit down and work on meal prep. This is a more challenging diet to work with, and figuring out the meals at the last minute will not be as easy as we may like. We need to really think about what we want to make and have it all in front of us ahead of time. When we do this, we can figure out our macronutrients and the right amount of variety. And it is a whole lot easier.

Think about it this way; when you are home from a long day at work and the kids are hungry and bouncing around, do you want to scramble around and hope that you are able to find the right ingredients to throw together a meal at the last minute? Or would it be better to just take something out of the fridge or the freezer, heat it up, and then dinner is made? And even better, you will know that it fits on the vegan diet so that you won't be questioning yourself along the way? This is possible when you work with your own meal prep program. Let's take a look now at a few of the steps you can take to see more success with meal planning and how it can be a simple process to work with.

Learn About Your Diet Plan

The first step that we need to take here is to learn more about our diet plan that we want to use. The vegan diet is a very healthy meal plan that we are able to work with, and you will quickly see how it is going to provide you with a lot of health benefits. We took some time to talk about the vegan diet plan in this guidebook, but the more that you are able to learn about it, and the more you explore how this diet works and which foods are allowed and which ones you should avoid, the easier it is going to be to make it work.

There are a lot of parts that come with the vegan diet, and as you go through and try to make the right recipes and stick with this diet plan, you will find that a lot of questions will creep up. It is not uncommon to look at a diet plan and wonder if one food or another will count for using it. Do some research and get a good understanding of what is allowed on the vegan diet so you can use it the right way.

Decide How Many Meals to Plan

This one is really going to depend on you and how much you want to get into all of this. Some people decide to just start with a few easy dinners to get the hang of it. Some want to plan out all of their meals and snacks each day of the week so they can grab and go without having to think about it. And some will try to do this for just a week, and others will do a few weeks or even a whole month so that they have some easy meals to put in the freezer and pull out when they need it.

You need to decide what is going to be the best for your own needs. This is going to let you know more about the different meals that you would like to create along the way. If you just want to do suppers, and you will just have oatmeal for breakfast, for example, then that may allow you to make some more meals at a time. Either way, knowing what meals you want to work with will ensure that you are set and will be able to pick out the right recipes for your needs.

Pick Out the Recipes You Want to Use

Once you know a bit more about the vegan diet and you have a good idea about which meals you need help with and how many you are going to prepare ahead of time, it is now time for you to go through and pick out which recipes you would like to add to your meal plan. Make sure to go with options that have a lot of variety in them. You do not want to get into the middle of your meal plan and start feeling bored with the foods you consume.

There are many different options that you can choose from when it comes to delicious vegan meals that will provide you with the nutrition and more that you are looking for. You will find that there are many tasty options for meals to go within this guidebook, along with other books and even online with a simple search. Go ahead and save a bunch of them because it is easy to switch a few backs and forth as you make meal plans throughout the next few weeks.

Write Down Shopping List and Hit the Store

As you are going through all of the recipes you want to create on this kind of diet plan, make sure you write out the ingredients. You can get a sheet that separates these all out into different categories to make it easier, or just write them out as you go and organize them later. Ensure that you get all of the ingredients written down and the right amounts so that you do not have to guess later and don't end up getting too much or too little.

Adding in some more organization to this process is going to make things a lot easier to handle. This will ensure that we are able to get some good results and save time at the grocery store. Once you are ready to head on over to the store, make sure that you stick to your list. Going off the list is not only going to cost you more at the store, but it is also going to make it more likely that you will pick up something that is unhealthy, whether it is part of the vegan diet or not. Stick with the list, and you will always have exactly what you need when you work on this kind of diet plan.

Prepare the Ingredients

When you get home from the grocery store, it is time to prepare the ingredients. The way you do this will depend on what kinds of foods you are trying to work with along the way. If you have a lot of produce, then go through and slice them all up and put them into small containers or into little baggies, so they are all together. If you are really organized and ready for the challenge, you can go through and separate them out based on how much is needed in the recipe. It is fine to go through and just add all of the same types into one container and sort them out later when making the recipes.

You may find that after grocery shopping, the idea of making all of these meals is going to be a challenge, and you may want to separate it out a little bit into two days. You can still go through and prepare the produce and other items so that when it is time to cook, whether it is that day or another day, you will have it all organized and ready to go for your own needs. Slice and dice now so that you can go right to the cooking later.

Make the Meals

Once you have gotten the recipes set up and all of the food prepared to go, this process should be easier. Always start with the things that will take the longest to make and work your way backward. This will ensure that you can keep moving and won't ever have to wait for something in the process. All of the cold meals you are making, such as sandwiches or salads, should be done last to prepare them while all of the other things are baking.

Keep some containers out as well, the ones you plan to use to store some of the meals when they are done. Think about when you will use each of these and how long you plan to hold onto them before eating. If it is more than a few days, then put those meals into the freezer to keep them safe. The amount of time that this process will take really depends on how many days of meals and how many meals a day you would like to prepare. Start with just a week or a few meals to see what the process is about to make things easier.

Storing and Reheating

When the meals are all done and created, you will find that it is time to store them. The way that your store will depend on how far the process goes and how long you plan to use the meals. If you are only meal planning for a few days, you may be fine storing the foods in the fridge for that short amount of time. But if you want it to be available just on your busy nights or don't plan to use it for a few weeks, it is best to put it into the freezer.

When you are making the meal, try to determine how long you need to store it. If it is just a few days, putting it into a few Tupperware containers should be enough for your work. You can finish making the meals, or even just cutting up the fruits and vegetables, then putting them in the fridge, ready to grab and run off when you want.

On the other hand, if you are looking to store the food to have ready over the next week, or even the next month, then you will need to plan a bit more. Get some containers that can hold onto the meals and be left in the freezer for some amount of time. You can then add the food to these containers, allow them to have some time to cool down after cooking, and then add them to the freezer. Make sure to add a label to each of these. This will ensure that you are able to remember what is in each of the pans or containers when you take a look at them in the freezer.

The next part is where some of the planning is going to come into play. You will need to pull out some of the foods ahead of time to help them defrost if they have been put into the freezer. If you pull them out ten minutes before you need them, it is going to take a long time to get them nice and warm, and you will be frustrated. Knowing what you are going to eat each day of the week, and planning in that manner, is going to make things so much easier overall. You can pull out a few days' worths of food to defrost slowly in the fridge, and then they will be ready to heat up when the time comes.

Meal planning is a process that takes a bit of time, and it is not always as simple and easy as we may hope. It is not something that we are able to get done within just a few minutes, either. Instead, it is something that we need to really think about and plan out to get it all to fit together. But when we can do all of that, it will really make things easier on us overall and ensure that we will see a lot more success when we go on this kind of diet plan.

PART 2
GETTING READY WITH THE MEAL PLAN

Chapter 5 - Your Weight Loss Meal Prep Program

The next thing that we need to take a look at here is how we can use the idea of meal prepping and meal planning to help us lose weight. Going on the vegan diet can be one of the best ways to lose weight and feel amazing, but you will also find that it is really hard to follow if you do not develop a plan. If you are good at planning and think through some of your work ahead of time, you will find that it is a great diet plan. But without meal planning, you are going to spend too much time at home worrying about what to eat on for support or another meal way too often, and you will give up because you are too worn out and tired.

When it comes to eating healthy to lose weight, failing to plan is the same as planning to fail. You can spend all day long exercising and doing all of the other things right, but if you are not consuming the right types of foods, or you are eating too much of the bad ones, you will find that all of the hard work in the world is not going to be shown off or on the scale.

Think about some of the thought and effort that you are able to put into your workouts. You think about what to wear, what workouts you are going to do, how intense and for how long, and what songs you want to add to the playlist. Doesn't it make sense that your nutrition should have a big impact on your weight as well and that you need to take some time to plan it out ahead of time as well?

Meal planning is going to be one of the main tools that you can use to achieve some of your own weight loss goals. Prepping your food ahead of time, whether that means that you are chopping up the fruits and vegetables that you want to use regularly for the week, putting together some salads in a jar for the week, or doing extra batches of things and freezing them for later, you will find that meal planning is going to be one of the best options for your needs.

There are a lot of reasons that meal planning is going to be a good thing for you to try, especially when you are on the vegan diet and when you want to be able to lose a lot of weight quickly. Some of the different ways that meal planning can be good for you include the following:

1. ***It can save you from the takeout trap.***
We have all been in this situation. We are tired, running low on time, and we are getting really hungry and angry at the same time. With all of these strikes going against you, you are going to be so much more vulnerable to the song of the fast-food or the pizza apps that can make life easier. After all, the convenience industry's whole idea is designed to help cater to those who don't believe that they have the energy or the time to cook.

Meal planning is a nice option to go with because it is going to throw out all of those excuses ahead of time. When you have a lot of healthy meals that are prepped and all ready to go for you, some of the takeout options go from being a necessary evil to something that you do not need at all.

2. *It can save a lot of time.*

Spending a few hours during the week in the kitchen will not exactly top the list of our favorite ways to spend an afternoon. But you will find that it can help you reap way more than a culinary reward from that one longer chunk of time than you would spending even half an hour cooking each evening during the week. It is possible to make a few weeks of meals in that sitting, and just have to throw it into the oven and have it ready throughout the whole week.

If you are a bit scared by the thought of trying to get all those meals done in one day, then it is time to spend some time here doing smaller tasks. You could start out your meal prep with some of the tasks like marinating chicken breasts or chopping onions. This is going to work with making things easier, even if it doesn't do all of the things that you need later. That way, when you are going through a stressful day, you will not allow it to ruin your healthy intentions along the way.

3. *Your snacks will be a lot smarter.*

There are those days when we are all good, and we start out on a positive path, patting ourselves on the back for eating a nutritious breakfast and a pretty good lunch. And then we get to the middle of the afternoon, and that sugar craving is going to send us right to the vending machine or a cookie jar, and that is not going to be good for our health.

We have to remember here that meal prep isn't going always to be the elaborate entrees. It is a chance to go through and plan some nutritious bites to have in between meals to don't end up ruining our whole diet with the hunger cravings that we have during snack time. Creating a few options that you can keep on hand to help with all of this and provide yourself with a natural vegan snack that will be so good for you.

4. *It can take out the impulse buys.*

When you are not on one of these meal plans, you will find that it is easier to add unplanned and unnecessary additions to your grocery cart that will add to your budget and can make it really hard to stick with your weight loss goals. Creating a meal plan can then help to make a simple grocery list. You can make that list and only purchase the items that are on it, nothing else. This ensures that you just get healthy and nutritious meals and nothing else.

5. *Portion control is easier with this.*

There is nothing better to focus on than portion control for those who are on a good weight loss journey. When you are eating at a restaurant or using other methods to help you out, this can be hard. But meal prepping can make it so much easier to keep your portions under control. For weight management, you will find that portion sizes will be one of the most important things you can follow. It helps you make sure you are not taking on too many calories, fat, sodium, or more.

The typical American is taking on so much more than they need. Especially when we are eating out, the portion sizes have easily doubled or tripled through the years. If you do meal prepping and ensure that you do some good portion control, you are more in control of the amounts you take in, which can do wonders to lose weight and cut out the calories effortlessly.

There are so many benefits that come with using the meal planning techniques for working on the vegan diet. When we can do it properly, you will find that the vegan diet is going to be easier to follow and can lead to a lot of natural and quick weight loss in the process.

CHAPTER 6 - ORGANIZING YOUR SHOPPING LIST

One of the things that we can do on this journey to ensure that we see the best results is to get some of our own grocery shopping lists all done. There are a lot of different ways that we can organize our list, but the more we think it out ahead of time, the more we can ensure that we will get into the store and out with all of the ingredients that we really need and none of the ones that don't fit with our diet plan. It is also a good way to make sure that we can speed up the time it takes to be at the grocery store, and that is always good news.

The first thing that we need to do is make the shopping list. But it is kind of hard to make a shopping list without a good idea of the recipes that we need to use and want to rely on for the next week. Some people decide to go through the coupons and the store ads ahead of time and pick out a few recipes that look good based on the sales. If you are really into saving money and not wasting it, then this is a good idea. If this is one of the first times you have done any kind of meal planning, you may want to keep it a little bit easier and just pick out some of the recipes that sound good.

Remember that we are on the vegan diet plan, so pick out recipes that will fit with this. You can look through cookbooks, ask friends and family for some ideas, and even go online. There are many great recipes, including the ones at the end of this guidebook, that you can use to help you get started. As you find the ones that you like, make sure to mark them in some manner so that you can remember where they are, and then go through and write it down on your calendar so you remember which day of your meal plan you would like to have it on.

As you find the recipes you want to work with, make sure to write down the ingredients and how much of each you would like to work with. You can have these out of order for now. We are simply writing a few down to make sure that we have the necessary ingredients and don't forget anything. The organization doesn't have to be there right from the start because we can work on that later. Just get it all written down for the desired number of meals that you want.

When this part is done, you should have a nice list and all of the meals written down into your meal plan. Now it is time to get organized. You don't want to run back and forth to the bread aisle, for example, because you need a loaf of bread, some buns, and some tortilla shells, but you wrote them down on different parts of the list, so they were not right together. This is a hassle and can really cause some pain when you go to the grocery store.

If you can, try to go through and bring them into order in some manner. You can do this based on the aisle they are in based on your store, or even the food group they are in. you can have protein sources together, produce together, grains together and so on. Pick the method that is going to make the most sense for what you are doing at this time. You want the organization as much as possible.

If you are doing online ordering, this can be even easier. Then you do not even need to organize the list at all. This can be a way to speed things up and saves you from spending that much time at the store at all. If this is offered in your area, it is something to give a try because it is going to make things a whole lot easier and saves you some time.

When you are in the store, make sure that you stick with the list that you made. Going off it can add in many unhealthy items that you do not need at the store and make the cost go up. The vegan diet is sometimes a bit more expensive than some of the other diet plans that are out there, so having a method to keep the costs down, such as making a grocery list and sticking with it, can be one of the best ways to make this work for you.

And that is it. Making your own shopping list is not something that has to be very difficult and take up all of your time. You just need to have a plan and go through it one step at a time. When you are able to do this, it is a whole lot easier to see some good results in the process, and you will get in and out of the grocery store with all of the items that you need and none of the ones that are just extras and won't help you stay on your goals.

Week 1

Day 1:
Breakfast: Almond explosion
Snack: Hazelnut and chocolate bars
Lunch: Lentil, lemon, and mushroom salad
Snack: Sunflower Protein Bars
Dinner: Black bean and quinoa burgers

Day 2:
Breakfast: Powerhouse protein shake
Snack: No-bake almond rice treats
Lunch: Sweet potato and black bean protein salad
Snack: overnight cookie dough oats
Dinner: Stuffed Indian Eggplant

Day 3:
Breakfast: Almond Protein Shake
Snack: matcha energy balls
Lunch: Southwest Style Salad

Snack: Lemon-lime pie bars
Dinner: Sweet potato sushi

Day 4:
Breakfast: Cranberry Protein Shake
Snack: mocha chocolate brownie bars
Lunch: Cuban Tempeh Buddha Bowl
Snack: Nutty blueberry snack bars
Dinner Tofu Cacciatore

Day 5:
Breakfast: Avocado Protein Shake
Snack: Cranberry vanilla protein bars
Lunch: Shaved Brussel Sprouts Salad
Snack: Spicy Chickpea poppers
Dinner: High Protein Black Bean Dip

Shopping List for Week 1:

1. 1 package brown rice syrup
2. 1 package cashew butter
3. 1 package cocoa powder
4. 1 package of hazelnuts
5. 1 package of chocolate-flavored protein powder
6. 1 package of vanilla vegan protein powder
7. 1 package of peanut butter
8. 1 package of almonds
9. 1 package of raisins
10. 1 package of oatmeal
11. 2 packages of almond milk, unsweetened
12. 1 package of nutmeg
13. 1 package of cinnamon
14. 1 package of vanilla
15. 1 package of sunflower butter
16. 1 bottle of maple syrup
17. 1 package of puffy rice cereal
18. 2 packages of oats
19. 1 package arugula

20. 1 package cilantro
21. 1 lemon
22. 1 package chili flakes
23. 1 package garlic powder
24. 1 bottle olive oil
25. 9 purpose or sweet onions
26. 1 package mushrooms
27. 1 package lentils
28. 1 package spirulina
29. 1 package kale
30. 1 package spinach
31. 1 pineapple
32. 2 green apples
33. 1 package of lettuce
34. 1 package of pepper
35. 1 package of paprika powder
36. 1 package red pepper lakes
37. 1 package of flour, whole wheat
38. 1 garlic head
39. 2 green and 2 red bell peppers
40. 1 package of quinoa
41. 3 packages of black beans
42. 1 package salt
43. 1 package of onion powder
44. 2 cans chickpeas
45. 1 package dried cranberries
46. 1 package walnuts
47. 1 package slivered almonds
48. 1 package Brussels sprouts
49. 1 package balsamic vinegar
50. 28 ounces of diced tomatoes
51. 1 package carrots
52. 1 package dried blueberries
53. 14 oz. tempeh
54. 1 package basmati rice
55. 1 package coffee, brewed
56. 1 bottle of coconut milk
57. 1 package hemp seeds

58. 1 banana
59. 1 package cranberries
60. 1 package tamari
61. 1 package agave nectar
62. 1 package rice vinegar
63. 1 package nori sheets
64. 2 packages of silken tofu
65. 1 package of sunflower seeds
66. 1 package pecans
67. 1 package chia seeds
68. 1 bottle of vinegar
69. 1 package chili powder
70. 1 package corn
71. 3 avocados
72. 7 cherry tomatoes
73. 1 package of mixed greens
74. 1 package garbanzo beans
75. 1 package matcha powder
76. 1 package dates
77. 1 package pistachios
78. 1 package cashews, raw
79. 1 package coconut milk
80. 1 bottle of soymilk
81. 1 package turmeric
82. 1 package cumin
83. 1 package coconut sugar
84. 2 packages tomato paste
85. 3 Roma tomatoes
86. 6 eggplants
87. 1 package flaxseed
88. 1 package parsley
89. 1 package cayenne
90. 1 sweet potato
91. 1 package, coconut shredded
92. 1 package almond butter
93. 1 package protein powder, no flavor
94. 1 bottle of coconut water.

Week 2

Day 1:
Breakfast: Banana protein punch
Snack: Chocolate and zucchini muffins
Lunch: Colorful protein salad
Snack: Energy Crackers
Dinner: Mango-Tempeh Wraps

Day 2:
Breakfast: Almond protein shake
Snack: sunflower protein bars
Lunch: Creamy squash pizza
Snack: chewy almond butter balls
Dinner: Edamame and Ginger Salad

Day 3:
Breakfast: Cranberry Protein Shake
Snack: Overnight Cookie Dough Oats
Lunch: Super Summer Salad
Dinner: Nutty Blueberry Snack Squares
Dinner: Sweet potato chili

Day 4:
Breakfast: Avocado Protein Shake
Snack: Peanut butter and banana cookies
Lunch: Vegan Mushroom pho
Snack: Almond and date bars.
Diner: Ruby Red Beet Burgers

Day 5:
Breakfast: Almond and date protein bars
Snack: Tropical protein smoothie
Lunch: Lasagna fungo
Snack: Savory sweet lentil bites
Dinner Portobello burgers

Shopping List for Week 2:

1. 1 package onion flakes
2. 1 package chia seeds
3. 1 package flax seeds
4. 1 lemon
5. 10 carrots
6. 1 package kale
7. 1 package of cabbage, green or purple
8. 1 head of garlic
9. 1 package green onions
10. 1 package navy beans
11. 1 package vanilla
12. 1 thing of nutmeg
13. 1 thing of cinnamon
14. 1 thing baking powder
15. 1 bottle or carton of almond milk
16. 1 package of chocolate chips, vegan
17. 1 zucchini
18. 1 package of maple syrup
19. 1 jar of applesauce
20. 7 bananas
21. 1 thing olive oil
22. 1 thing of coconut oil
23. 1 thing of pepper
24. 2 quinoa packages
25. 1 thing salt
26. 1 bottle or carton of oat milk
27. 3 things of almonds
28. 1 package chocolate protein powder
29. 1 package vanilla protein powder
30. 1 thing of chili powder
31. 2 buns or wraps
32. 1 thing of mushrooms, portobello
33. 1 thing of sunflower seeds
34. 1 thing of allspice
35. 1 thing of nutritional yeast
36. 1 thing of hummus
37. 1 thing of lasagna noodles

38. 1 thing of hemp seeds
39. 1 carton of blueberries
40. 1 orang
41. 1 thing of parsley
42. 1 thing of balsamic vinegar
43. 1 thing of garbanzo beans
44. 2 beets
45. 1 package cranberries, dried
46. 1 thing bean sprouts, raw
47. 1 package of rice noodles
48. 1 thing of hoisin sauce
49. 1 thing of mushrooms
50. 1 thing cocoa nibs
51. 1 carton coconut milk
52. 1 thing cacao powder
53. 4 packages of tofu
54. 2 sweet potatoes
55. 1 can diced tomatoes with green chilis
56. 1 thing of sweet onions
57. 1 package of dried blueberries
58. 1 package chickpeas
59. 1 thing of radishes
60. 1 bushel of Brussels sprouts
61. 1 thing of beans, red kidney
62. 1 package of basil
63. 1 package of rolled oats
64. 1 lime
65. 1 carton of orange juice
66. 1 bottle sesame oil
67. 1 package of ginger
68. 2 packages of green lentils
69. 1 thing of edamame
70. 1 thing of mint
71. 3 avocados
72. 1 package puffy rice cereal
73. 1 package of vanilla
74. 1 jar of almond butter
75. 1 thing of carb chips

76. 1 thing of onion powder
77. 1 onion, purple
78. 1 thing of French lentils
79. 1 head of broccoli
80. 1 red and one green bell pepper
81. 1 thing of paprika
82. 1 thing of cumin
83. 1 thing of oregano
84. Red pepper flakes
85. 2 squash, butternut
86. Cocoa powder
87. 1 carton of milk, soy
88. 1 thing of garlic powder
89. 1 lettuce head
90. 3 mangoes
91. 1 package sweet chili sauce
92. 2 tempeh packages
93. Paprika powder
94. 1 thing of sesame seeds
95. 2 things of cashews
96. 2 things of pumpkin seeds
97. 2 things of peanuts

Week 3

Day 1:
Breakfast: cinnamon and apple protein smoothie
Snack: Lemon-lime pie bars
Lunch: Portobello burritos
Snack: Lentil radish salad
Dinner: Mushroom madness stroganoff

Day 2:
Breakfast: Candied protein trail mix
Snack: Cake batter smoothie
Lunch: Creamy squash pizza
Snack: Chocolate and zucchini muffins
Dinner: Sweet and Sour Tofu

Day 3:
Breakfast; Chewy Almond butter balls
Snack: Energy Crackers
Lunch: Moroccan eggplant stew
Snack: Mocha chocolate brownie bars
Dinner: Taco Tempeh Salad

Day 4:
Breakfast: Banana Protein Punch
Snack: Sunflower Protein Bars
Lunch: Ratatouille
Snack: Spicy chickpea poppers
Dinner: BBQ Greens and Grits

Day 5:
Breakfast: Avocado Chia Protein Shake
Snack: Cranberry Vanilla Protein Bars
Lunch: Roasted Almond Protein Salad
Snack: Lemon Lime Pie Bars
Dinner: Sweet Potato Quesadillas

1. Cherry tomatoes, 3
2. Radishes, 2
3. Silken tofu, 1 package
4. Brown lentils, 1 package
5. Chickpeas, 1 package
6. Sesame oil, 1 container
7. Miso paste, 1 package
8. Maple syrup, 1 bottle
9. Flour, 1 package
10. Jalapeno, 1
11. Red onion, 1
12. Tomatoes, 1 container
13. Cilantro, 1 bunch
14. Avocados, 3
15. Potatoes, 2
16. Portobello mushrooms, 1 package
17. Lemons, 2
18. Dates, 1 package
19. Raw cashews, 2 packages
20. Pecans, 2 containers
21. Chia seeds, 2 containers
22. Coconut oil, 1 container
23. Olive oil, 1 bottle
24. Chocolate protein powder, 1 package
25. Vanilla protein powder, 1 package
26. Pepper
27. Salt
28. Cinnamon, 1 container
29. Coconut milk, 2 cartons
30. Green apple, 1
31. Garlic powder
32. Chickpeas, 2 cans
33. Basil, 1 bunch
34. Yellow squash, 1
35. Fennel seeds, 1 package
36. Heirloom tomatoes, 2
37. Sunflower butter, 1 container

38. Oat milk, 1 carton
39. Kale, 1 bunch
40. Lime, 1
41. Jalapeno, 1
42. Tempeh, 2 packages
43. Black beans, 1 package
44. Brewed coffee, 1 package
45. Agave nectar, 1 package
46. Cocoa powder, 1 package
47. Sweet onions, 1 package
48. Tomato sauce, 1 package
49. Green lentils, 1 package
50. Allspice, 1 package
51. Eggplants, 2
52. Turmeric, 1 package
53. Golden raisins, 1 package
54. Garbanzo beans, 1 package
55. Peanuts, 1 package
56. Onion flakes
57. Flaxseeds, 1 container
58. Almond butter, 1 jar
59. Puffy rice cereal, 1 package
60. Carob chips, 1 package
61. Coconut sugar, 1 package
62. Cornstarch, 1 package
63. Drained tofu, 2 packages
64. Soy sauce, 1 package
65. Rice vinegar, 1 bottle
66. Bell pepper, red, 1
67. Green bell peppers, 2
68. White onions, 2
69. Ginger root, 1
70. Pineapple, 1
71. Quinoa, 2 packages
72. Zucchini, 2
73. Baking powder, 1
74. Applesauce, 1 jar
75. Purple onions, 2

76. Red pepper flakes, 1 package
77. Oregano, 1 package
78. Paprika, 1 package
79. Cumin, 1 package
80. Onion powder, 1 package
81. Garlic, 1 head
82. French green lentils, 1 package
83. Broccoli, 1 head
84. Butternut squash, 2
85. Almond milk, 2 cartons
86. Vanilla, 1
87. Oats, 2 packages
88. Cashew butter, 1 jar
89. Bananas, 5
90. Nutmeg, 1
91. Walnuts, 2 containers
92. Almonds, 3 containers
93. Apple cider vinegar, 1 bottle
94. Spinach, 2 packages
95. Thyme
96. Mushrooms, 1 package
97. Tomato paste, 1 package
98. Tamari sauce, 1 package
99. Almond flour, 1 package
100. Noodles, 1 package
101. Sesame seeds, 1 package.
102. Sweet potato, 1
103. Rice, 1 package
104. Navy beans, 1
105. Dried cranberries, 1
106. The coconut that is shredded, 1
107. Peanut butter, 1 jar
108. Smoked paprika, 1
109. Grits, 1
110. Collard greens, 1
111. Cayenne, 1

Week 4

Day 1:
Breakfast: Cinnamon and apple protein smoothie
Snack Nutty, blueberry snack squares.
Lunch: Stuffed Eggplant
Dinner: Savory Sweet Lentil Bites
Dinner: Teriyaki Tofu Wraps

Day 2:
Breakfast: Mocha Chocolate Brownie Bars
Snack: Cookie Dough Oats
Lunch: Satay Tempeh
Snack: Banana Protein Punch
Dinner: Tex-Mex Tofu and Beans

Day 3:
Breakfast: Almond Explosion
Snack: Matcha Energy Balls
Lunch: Stuffed Sweet Potatoes
Snack: Sunflower Protein Bars
Dinner: Red Beans and Rice

Day 4:
Breakfast; Cranberry Protein Shake
Snack: Hazelnut and Chocolate Protein Bars
Lunch: Coconut Tofu Curry
Snack Almond and date protein bars
Dinner: Tahini Falafels

Day 5:
Breakfast: Almond Protein Shake
Snack: Energy Crackers
Lunch: Black Bean Dip
Snack: Lemon Lime Pie Bars
Dinner: Baked Enchilada Bowls

Shopping List for Week 4

1. White onion, 1
2. Almond butter, 1 jar
3. Shredded coconut, 1 package
4. Sunflower seeds, 1 package
5. Allspice, 1 package
6. Coconut oil, 1 container
7. Green lentils,1 package
8. Green bell peppers,5
9. Turmeric, 1 thing
10. Cumin, 1 thing
11. Coconut sugar, 1 package
12. Tomato paste, 1 can
13. Garlic, 1 head
14. Spinach, 1 package
15. Olive oil, 1 container
16. Purple onions, 3
17. Roma tomatoes, 3
18. Eggplants, 6
19. Black beans, 3 packages
20. Pepper
21. Salt
22. Dried blueberries, 1 package
23. Maple syrup, 1 bottle
24. Puffy rice cereals, 1 package
25. Cashews, 4 packages with 2 raw
26. Almonds, 2 packages with 1 raw
27. Green apple, 1
28. Chocolate protein powder, 1 package
29. Vanilla protein powder,1 package
30. Cinnamon, 1 thing
31. Coconut milk, 1 carton
32. Nutritional yeast, 1
33. Apple vinegar, 1 bottle
34. Flour, 1 package
35. Oregano, 1
36. MCT oil, 1 bottle
37. Sweet potato,1

38. Pecans, 1 container
39. Onion powder, 1 thing
40. Pumpkinseeds, 1 package
41. Onion flakes, 1
42. Soymilk, 1 carton
43. Broccoli,1 head
44. Tahini, 1 package
45. Chickpeas, 1 package
46. Dried cranberries, 1 package
47. Applesauce, 1 jar
48. Tomatoes, 2
49. Coconut milk, 1 can
50. Peas, 1 package
51. Turmeric,1 package
52. Cashew butter, 1 jar
53. Curry powder 1 thing
54. Brown rice syrup, 1 bottle
55. Hemp seeds, 1 package
56. Chia seeds, 1 package
57. Cranberries, 1
58. Celery ribs, 1
59. Parsley flakes, 1
60. Basil, 1
61. Cauliflower, 1
62. Red beans, 1
63. Sunflower butter, 1 jar
64. Pistachios, 1 package
65. Matcha powder, 1
66. Hazelnuts, 1
67. Dates, 1
68. Raisins, 1
69. Lemons, 2
70. Chili powder,1
71. Avocado,1
72. Paprika, 1
73. Tofu, 1
74. Brown rice, 1
75. Banana, 3

76. Oat milk, 1 carton
77. Purple cabbage, 1
78. Cauliflower rice, 1
79. Tempeh, 2
80. Red pepper flakes, 1
81. Rice vinegar, 1 bottle
82. Ginger root, 1
83. Peanut butter, 1 jar
84. Flaxseeds, 1
85. Almond milk, 2 cartons
86. Agave nectar, 1 package
87. Brewed coffee, 1 package
88. Vanilla,1
89. Nutmeg
90. Oats, 2
91. Pineapple, 1
92. Sesame seeds,1
93. Lettuce, 1 package
94. Sesame oil, 1 bottle,
95. Soy sauce, 1 bottle.

PART 3

THE RECIPES

Cinnamon and Apple Protein Smoothie

Ingredients:

Matcha powder (2 tsp.)
Ice cubes (3)
Cinnamon (.5 tsp.)
Coconut milk (1 c.)
Vegan protein powder, vanilla (2 scoops)
Apple, green ad chopped (1)

Directions:

1. Take out your blender and add all of the ingredients above inside. Let these blend together for about 2 minutes.
2. When this is done, move the shake to a big cup or to a shaker. Top it all with some of the cinnamon powder and enjoy.

***

Tropical Protein Smoothie

Ingredients:
Ice cubes (6)
Guarana (1 tsp.)
Hemp seeds (1 Tbsp.)
Vegan protein powder, choose chocolate or vanilla (2 scoops)
blueberries (.5 c.)
Mango chunks (1 c)
Peeled and parted orange (1)

Directions:
1. To start this recipe, bring out your blender and add in all of your ingredients, along with the guarana.
2. Put the lid on top and then let this mix for a few minutes. After two minutes, you can transfer the shake to a shaker or a cup and enjoy it.

***

Cranberry Protein Shake

Ingredients:
Ice cubes (4)
Coconut milk (2 c.)
Hemp seeds (.25 c.)
Chia seeds (.25 c.)
Banana (1)
Vegan protein powder, vanilla or chocolate (2 scoops)
Cranberries (.25 c.)

Directions:
1. Go through and soak the chia seeds for a few hours before starting this recipe.
2. When the chia seeds are done with soaking, you can add them along with the rest of the ingredients into your blender.
3. Add the lid on top of the blender and then blend all of these together for a few minutes.
4. When this is done, move the mixture to some large cups and serve.

Strawberry and Orange Smoothie

Ingredients:
Ice cubes (2)
Vanilla vegan protein powder (3 scoops)
Banana (1)
Orange (1)
Strawberries (10)
Coconut milk (2 c.)

Directions:
1. To start this recipe, bring out a blender and add in all of the ingredients that we are using.
2. Add the lid on top of the blender and let the ingredients mix together for a few minutes.
3. When the two minutes are up, move this over to a big cup and then serve.

***

Powerhouse Protein Shake

Ingredients:
Unflavored protein powder (2 scoops)
Coconut water (1 c.)
Spirulina (1 tsp)
Drained and rinsed spinach (1 c.)
Chopped kale (1 c.)
Pineapple chunks (1 c.)
Chopped green apple (2)

Directions:
1. Take all of the ingredients and add them to your prepared blender.
2. Put the lid on top of the blender and then let these mix together for about 2 minutes.
3. After that is done, move to a large cup and ten enjoy.

***

Avocado Protein Shake

Ingredients:
Cacao powder (2 tsp.)
Ice cubes (3)
Water (1 c.)
Chocolate protein powder (2 scoops)
Peanut butter (1.5 Tbsp.)
Pitted and peeled avocado (.5)
Coconut milk (1 c.)
Dry chia seeds (.25 c.)

Directions:
1. Take a bit of time before making this to soak the chia seeds. After a few hours, you can drain out the water that is left.
2. Add in these chia seeds and any of the other ingredients to your blender. Blend these for a few minutes to make them smooth.
3. Move the shake to a bit cup and then add a bit of cacao powder on top before serving.

***

Almond Protein Shake

Ingredients:
Cacao powder (1 tsp.)
Ice cubes (4)
Chocolate protein powder (2 scoops)
Coconut oil (1 Tbsp.)
Maple syrup (1 tsp.)
Almonds (3 Tbsp)
Soymilk (1.5 c.)

Directions:
1. Bring out your blender, and then add all of the ingredients inside.
2. Blend all of the ingredients together for a few minutes. And when this is done, add the shake to a large shaker or cup and then serve.

Oatmeal Protein Mix

Ingredients:
Peanut butter (2 Tbsp.)
Ice cubes (2)
Almond milk (1 c.)
Almonds (.25 c.)
Maple syrup (.5 tsp.)
Cinnamon (.5 tsp.)
Chocolate vegan protein powder (3 scoops)
Oatmeal, dry (1 c.)

Directions:
1. Bring out your blender and add in all of the ingredients that are listed above.
2. When this is ready, add the lid to the top of the blender and mix the ingredients together for two minutes.
3. When that is done, move to a big cup or to your shaker before enjoying it.

***

Almond Explosion

Ingredients:
- ✓ Ice cubes (2)
- ✓ Cinnamon (.5 tsp.)
- ✓ Vanilla protein powder (3 scoops)
- ✓ Peanut butter (3 Tbsp.)
- ✓ Water (.5 c.)
- ✓ Almonds (.5 c.)
- ✓ Raisins (.5 c.)
- ✓ Dry oatmeal (.5 c.)
- ✓ Almond milk (1.5 c.)

Directions:
1. Take out your blender and get it all set up. When ready, you can add all of the ingredients to the blender.
2. Add the lid on top of the blender. Allow this to blend together for a few minutes.
3. After this time, transfer to a large cup. Add some ice cubes if you want to keep this cool or microwave for a nice treat.

Banana Protein Punch

Ingredients:
Maple syrup (1 Tbsp.)
Vegan protein powder, vanilla or chocolate (2 scoops)
Water (.5 c.)
Almonds (.5 c.)
Almond milk (1 c.)
Bananas (2)

Directions:
1. Take out the blender and get it all set up. Add in all of the ingredients above to your blender, and then blend them for a few minutes.
2. Pour this into a large cup or your shaker, and then enjoy it.

***

Pecan and Maple Granola

Ingredients:
- ✓ Ground cinnamon (.5 tsp.)
- ✓ Maple syrup (.25 c)
- ✓ Vanilla (1 tsp.)
- ✓ Pecan pieces (.25 c.)
- ✓ Rolled oats (1.5 c.)

Directions:
1. Turn on the oven to start this and give it time to heat up to 300 degrees. While the oven is heating up, take out a baking sheet and line it with some parchment paper.
2. Then, take out a big bowl and combine together the cinnamon, vanilla, maple syrup, pecan pieces, and the oats. Stir these until the pecan pieces and the oats are coated all the way through.
3. When those are combined, you can spread this mixture out onto the baking sheet that you prepared ad then make it into an even layer. Add to the oven to bake.
4. After about 20 minutes, with a check on them at ten minutes, the granola should be all done. Take these out of the oven and let them set on the counter to cool down for a bit before serving.

Overnight Oatmeal

Ingredients:

- ✓ Chia seeds (1 Tbsp.)
- ✓ Maple syrup (1 Tbsp.)
- ✓ Sliced banana (1)
- ✓ Pineapple chunks (.5 c.)
- ✓ Diced mango (.5 c.)
- ✓ Plant-based milk (2 c.)
- ✓ Rolled oats (2 c.)

Directions:

1. Bring out a big bowl and mix together the chia seeds, maple syrup, banana, pineapple, mango, milk, and oats.
2. When this is done, cover up the bowl and add it to the fridge. This needs to set for at least four hours, though leaving it to sit overnight is usually going to be the best.
3. The next morning you can take this out and serve.

***

Pumpkin Pie Oatmeal

Ingredients:

- ✓ Ground nutmeg (.25 tsp.)
- ✓ Ground cloves (.25 tsp.)
- ✓ Ground cinnamon (1 tsp.)
- ✓ Maple syrup (2 Tbsp.)
- ✓ Unsweetened pumpkin puree (1 c.)
- ✓ Oats (1 c.)
- ✓ Plant-based milk (3 c.)

Directions:

1. Brin gout a pan and heat it up on medium heat. Add the milk inside and then let this come to a boil.
2. When the milk is to a rolling boil, you can reduce the heat down to a low and then stir in the nutmeg, cloves, cinnamon, maple syrup, oats, and pumpkin puree.
3. When all of those are in the pot, cover it up and let these cook for a bit. You will want to stop and stir it every few minutes to help keep it mixed and make sure that none of the oatmeal can stick to the bottom.
4. After about half an hour, this mixture should be done. Pour it into a few bowls before serving.

Peanut Butter and Chocolate Quinoa

Ingredients:
Peanut powder (1 Tbsp.)
Cocoa powder (1 Tbsp.)
Maple syrup (1 Tbsp.)
Cooked quinoa (2 c.)
Milk that is based on plants (1 c.)

Directions:
1. Take the time to cook up the quinoa. You can follow the instructions that are on the back of the box that came with it to make this easier.
2. When that is done, bring out another pan and heat it up. Add the milk inside and bring this to a boil as well.
3. When the milk is at a rolling boil, then it is time to reduce the heat a bit to a low setting before adding in the peanut powder, cocoa powder, maple syrup, and quinoa.
4. Cook these for a bit without the lid on top. After five minutes, with a constant stream of stirring the whole time, you can serve this mixture nice and warm.

Lentil and Mushroom Salad

Ingredients:

- ✓ Pepper
- ✓ Salt
- ✓ Arugula (.5 c.)
- ✓ Chopped cilantro (2 Tbsp.)
- ✓ Lemon juice (1 Tbsp.)
- ✓ Chili flakes (.25 tsp.)
- ✓ Garlic powder (2 Tbsp.)
- ✓ Olive oil (4 tsp.)
- ✓ Chopped purple onion (1 c.)
- ✓ Sliced mushrooms (3 c.)
- ✓ Vegetable broth (2 c.)
- ✓ Dry lentils (.5 c.)

Directions:

1. Take some time to sprout the lentils using the method of your choice. When that is done, take the vegetable stock and bring it to a boil in a pan on your stove.
2. Add the lentils to this boiling broth and then cover up the pan. Let these cook until the lentils start to get a bit tender.

3. After 5 minutes, you can take the pan off the heat and then drain the extra water.
4. Then add in a frying pan over high heat and then add in two tablespoons of olive oil. When that is warm, add in the chili flakes, garlic, and onions.
5. Cook this one until the onions start to turn translucent, which can take around ten minutes. Add the mushrooms to this and mix around well.
6. Continue to cook for a bit until the onions and mushrooms are done. Take the pan from the heat.
7. Mix the garlic, mushrooms, onions, and lentils in a big bowl. Add the lemon juice and then top with the rest of the oil. Toss or stir to make sure that it is combined well.
8. Serve this mixture over the arugula in a bowl, adding some of the pepper and salt to taste as you would like.

Sweet Potato and Black Bean Salad

Ingredients:

- ✓ Pepper
- ✓ Salt
- ✓ Parsley (.25 c.)
- ✓ Cayenne (.25 tsp.)
- ✓ Chili powder (.5 Tbsp.)
- ✓ Minced garlic (1 Tbsp.)
- ✓ Lime juice (2 Tbsp.)
- ✓ Olive oil (2 Tbsp.)
- ✓ Chopped purple onion (1 c.)
- ✓ Sweet potato (1)
- ✓ Spinach (4 c.)
- ✓ Dry black beans (1 c.)

Directions:

1. Take some time to preheat the black beans. Turn on the oven and let it heat up to 400 degrees.
2. Slice up the sweet potatoes into little cubes and then add to a bowl. Then add in the salt, olive oil, and onions.
3. Toss these ingredients around until the onions and sweet potatoes are completely coated and then add to a baking sheet that has been lined with some parchment paper. Make sure to spread them out in a single layer.
4. Add these to the oven and let them cook for a bit until the sweet potatoes start to become crispy and brown.
5. After 40 minutes, the potatoes and the rest of the mixture will be done. In the meantime, you can take out a bowl and combine the cayenne, chili powder, garlic, lime juice, and the rest of the olive oil.
6. When the potatoes are done, take them out of the oven and move them to the big bowl. Then top with the salt, parsley, and black beans. Toss these around to combine well.
7. Mix in the spinach and then serve.

***

Super Summer Salad

Ingredients:

For the dressing
- ✓ Avocado, diced (1)
- ✓ Water (.25 c.)
- ✓ Salt
- ✓ Chopped basil (.25 c.)
- ✓ Lemon juice (1 tsp.)
- ✓ Olive oil (1 Tbsp.)

For the salad
- ✓ Pepper
- ✓ Salt
- ✓ Dry chickpeas (.25 c.)
- ✓ Flaxseeds (1 tsp.)
- ✓ Red kidney beans (.25 c.)
- ✓ Sliced radishes (2)
- ✓ Chopped walnuts (1 Tbsp.)
- ✓ Brussel sprouts (2 c.)
- ✓ Shredded kale (4 c.)

Directions:

1. We can go through this and prepare the kidney beans and the chickpeas according to the method we like the moat.
2. Take out a small bowl and soak up the flax seeds for a few minutes or more. When that time is done, drain out the extra water.
3. Now it is time to prepare the dressing. To do this, bring out a blender and add in all the ingredients for the dressing, including half the avocado, lemon juice, salt, olive oil, and basil.
4. Pulse this at a low speed and add in some smaller amounts of water until the dressing is smooth and creamy, and then add to a bowl and set to the side.
5. Now it is time to bring out a big bowl and mix the rest of the avocado with the walnuts, radishes, kidney beans, kale, Brussel sprouts, kale, and chickpeas.
6. Serve this with the dressing and the flax seeds on top.

Roasted Almond Protein Salad

Ingredients:

- ✓ Chopped purple onion (.25 c.)
- ✓ Spinach (4 c.)
- ✓ Dry quinoa (.5 c.)
- ✓ Navy beans, dry (.5 c.)
- ✓ Dash of chili powder
- ✓ Cayenne (.5 tsp.)
- ✓ Paprika (.5 tsp.)
- ✓ Chickpeas dry (.5 c.)
- ✓ Salt
- ✓ Olive oil (1 tsp.)
- ✓ Whole almonds, raw (.5 c.)

Directions:

1. Take out a pan and add the water and quinoa to it. Cook the quinoa-based on the instructions on the box and then store it in the fridge when it is done.
2. Then you can go through the process of preparing the beans as well. When those are done, add them to the fridge as well.
3. Bring out a bowl and stir together the olive oil, salt, spices, and almonds and stir to make them nice and coated.
4. Take out a skillet and heat it up. When it is nice and warm, add the almond mixture to this. You can roast this while stirring the almonds around so that they can get browned all over. You may hear that it will crackle and pop a bit in the skillet, which is normal for this one.
5. After 5 minutes, making sure to stir around the whole time to prevent burning, you can turn off the heat and toss in the onions, cooked quinoa, beans, spinach, and more to the skillet. Stir it well before moving to a bowl.
6. Enjoy this salad with some of the dressing of your choice.

***

Lentil Radish Salad

Ingredients:
Dressing

- ✓ Pepper
- ✓ Salt
- ✓ Miso paste, white (1 Tbsp.)
- ✓ Sesame oil (.5 Tbsp.)
- ✓ Olive oil (1 Tbsp.)
- ✓ Maple syrup (1 Tbsp.)
- ✓ Water (1 Tbsp.)
- ✓ Lemon juice (1 Tbsp.)

For the salad

- ✓ Dry chickpeas (.5 c.)
- ✓ Brown lentils, dry (.25 c.)
- ✓ Silken tofu (14 oz.)
- ✓ Roasted sesame seeds (.25 c.)
- ✓ Halved cherry tomatoes (.5 c.)
- ✓ Mixed greens (5 c.)
- ✓ Sliced radishes (2)

Directions:
1. Take the time to prepare both the lentils and the chickpeas with the help of a favorite method.
2. When that is done, add all of the ingredients that we are using for the dressing into the food processor or blender. Mix this on a low setting until it is nice and smooth, adding in the water necessary to get it to your choice's right consistency.
3. Add some pepper and salt to taste and a bit more water to this to make it just right before setting it to the side.
4. Now it is time to cut the tofu into some smaller cubes. Then you can add this to a bowl with the tomatoes, radishes, chickpeas, mixed greens, and lentils.
5. Add in the dressing and then mix it all together. Top with some roasted sesame seeds and enjoy.

Southwest Salad

Ingredients:

- ✓ Vinegar (1 Tbsp.)
- ✓ Olive oil (2 tsp.)
- ✓ Pepper
- ✓ Salt
- ✓ Cumin (.25 tsp.)
- ✓ Chili powder (.5 tsp.)
- ✓ Sweet kernel corn (1 c.)
- ✓ Cubed avocado (1)
- ✓ Cherry tomatoes (1 c.)
- ✓ Chopped mixed greens (4 c.)
- ✓ Sliced red bell pepper (1)
- ✓ Diced purple onion (.5 c.)
- ✓ Dry chickpeas (.5 c.)
- ✓ Dry black beans (.5 c.)

Directions:

1. You can go through and use your favorite method in order to get the chickpeas and black beans all ready to go.
2. When this is done, you can bring out a big bowl and add all of the ingredients that we have above into it.
3. Toss the mix of spice and veggies together so they combine and mix well. Store or serve chilled with a bit of vinegar and olive oil over it all.

Shaved Brussel Sprout Salad

Ingredients:

Dressing

- ✓ Minced garlic (.5 Tbsp.)
- ✓ Olive oil (2 Tbsp.)
- ✓ Apple cider vinegar (2 Tbsp.)
- ✓ Maple syrup (1 Tbsp.)
- ✓ Brown mustard (1 Tbsp.)
- ✓ *For the Salad*
- ✓ Pepper
- ✓ Salt
- ✓ Dried cranberries (.5 c.)
- ✓ Crushed walnuts (.5 c.)
- ✓ Crushed almonds (.5 c.)
- ✓ Sour apple (1)
- ✓ Purple onion (1 c.)
- ✓ Brussel sprouts (2 c.)
- ✓ Dry chickpeas (.25 c.)
- ✓ Red kidney beans, dry (.5 c.)

Directions:

1. To start this recipe, start preparing the beans using one of your favorite methods.
2. When that is done, take out a bowl and combine together all of the ingredients that we are using for our dressing.
3. Add the dressing to the fridge and let it sit there for about an hour before you use it to serve.
4. When ready, you can take out a knife, mandolin, or grater and use it to thinly slice up your Brussel sprouts. You can repeat this same idea with the onion and the apple.
5. Now it is time to take out a big bowl and you can combine the nuts, cranberries, onions, apples, sprouts, beans, and chickpeas inside.
6. Sprinkle on some of the cold and prepared dressing to the salad and then serve with some pepper or salt to taste before enjoying.

***

Colorful Protein Power Salad

Ingredients:

- ✓ Pepper
- ✓ Salt
- ✓ Lemon juice (1 tsp.)
- ✓ Olive oil (2 Tbsp.)
- ✓ Shredded and chopped carrot (1 c.)
- ✓ Chopped kale (4 c.)
- ✓ Purple cabbage (3 c.)
- ✓ Minced garlic (2 tsp.)
- ✓ Chopped green onion (1)
- ✓ Dry navy beans (2 c.)
- ✓ Dry quinoa (.5 c.)

Directions:

1. Take out the quinoa and then follow the directions on the box to figure out how to make it the right way. Then you are able to use your favorite methods in order to prepare the beans.
2. When ready, you can take out a frying pan and heat up about a tablespoon of olive oil.
3. When this is warm, you can add in the cabbage, garlic, and chopped green onion. Let this heat up for a few minutes.
4. Add in the rest of the oil with the salt and the kale and then lower the heat and cover this up until it is wilted.
5. After another five minutes of cooking this, you can take the pan off the stove and set it to the side.
6. Take out a big bowl here and then add in the rest of the ingredients with your prepared cabbage and kale mixture. Add in some more pepper and salt if you would like, mixing until it is all distributed in the right manner.
7. Serve this with some of the dressing on top of each serving and then enjoy right away.

***

Edamame and Ginger Citrus Salad

Ingredients:

Dressing
- ✓ Sesame oil (.5 Tbsp.)
- ✓ Minced ginger (.5 tsp.)
- ✓ Maple syrup (.5 Tbsp.)
- ✓ Lime juice (1 tsp.)
- ✓ Orange juice (.25 c.)

For the Salad
- ✓ Sliced avocado (1)
- ✓ Pepper
- ✓ Salt
- ✓ Chopped mint (2 tsp.)
- ✓ Roasted sesame seeds (1 Tbsp.)
- ✓ Shelled edamame (1 c.)
- ✓ Chopped kale (4 c.)
- ✓ Shredded carrots (2 c.)
- ✓ Dry green lentils (.5 c.)

Directions:
1. Take out the lentils and then prepare them with the method that you like the most.
2. When that is done, you can bring out a bowl and combine the ginger, maple syrup, lime juices, and orange juice. Mix up with a whisk while adding in your sesame oil slowly.
3. When that is done, take out another bowl and add in the mint, sesame seeds, edamame, kale, carrot, and the cooked lentils.
4. Add the dressing and then stir it all together as well as possible so that the ingredients can be coated in an even manner. Store or serve with some of the avocado and a bit more mint before serving.

Vegan Mushroom Pho

Ingredients:

- ✓ Pepper
- ✓ Salt
- ✓ Chopped cabbage (1 c.)
- ✓ Chopped bok choy (1 c.)
- ✓ Matchstick carrots (1 c.)
- ✓ Raw bean sprouts (1 c.)
- ✓ Rice noodles (2 c.)
- ✓ Sesame oil (1 Tbsp.)
- ✓ Hoisin sauce (2 Tbsp.)
- ✓ Sliced mushrooms (3 c.)
- ✓ Olive oil (1 Tbsp.)
- ✓ Minced ginger (1 tsp.)
- ✓ Sliced green onions (3)
- ✓ Vegetable broth (6 c.)
- ✓ Drained firm tofu (14 oz.)

Directions:

1. Take the tofu out and cut it into some cubes before setting it to the side. Take out a pan, and then heat up the vegetable broth along with the ginger and the green onions.
2. Boil this for a minute before reducing the heat to a low setting. Cover with the lid and then let it simmer for a bit.
3. After 20 minutes, take out another pan and heat up the oil. Add in the sliced mushrooms to the pan and cook until they become soft.
4. Then add in the sesame oil, hoisin sauce, and tofu. Heat up the sauce and let it get nice and thick. After 5 minutes, you can take this off the heat.
5. Use the instructions on the package of the noodles to prepare the rice noodles. Top these noodles with some of the tofu mushroom mixture and some broth, and the bean sprouts.
6. Add in the carrots and then other ingredients as well if needed, and then serve warm.

Ruby Red Burger

Ingredients:
- ✓ Buns (6)
- ✓ Spinach washed and dried (2 c.)
- ✓ Pepper and salt
- ✓ Onion powder (2 tsp.)
- ✓ Chopped parsley (1 tsp.)
- ✓ Balsamic vinegar (1 Tbsp.)
- ✓ Garlic powder (2 Tbsp.)
- ✓ Olive oil (2 Tbsp.)
- ✓ Beets (2)
- ✓ Dry quinoa (.5 c.)
- ✓ Dry chickpeas (1 c.)

Directions:
1. Start this recipe by heating up the oven to 400 degrees. Take the time to prepare the quinoa and the chickpeas according to the method that you prefer.
2. While those are getting prepared, you can peel and then dice up the beats and add them to a bowl along with the onion powder and the olive oil.
3. Spread out these beets in a baking pan and then add it to the oven. After 10 minutes, the beets should be done. You can then take them out of the oven to cool down.
4. When they are nice and cool, take the beets off the baking sheet and add them into the food processor along with the quinoa pepper, garlic, parsley, salt vinegar, and chickpeas.
5. Pulse these ingredients for about half a minute to make them nice and crumble. Then you can use your hands to make six patties out of this mixture and add to a small pan.
6. Add these to the freezer for an hour until the patties are nice and firm. After that 60 minutes, take out a skillet and add in a bit of oil. Add the patties when it is warm.
7. These need to get browned on each side, which can take about 4 minutes on both sides.
8. Serve these with a bit of spinach on the buns that you chose.

Mango and Tempeh Wraps

Ingredients:
- ✓ Salt (.25 tsp)
- ✓ Lime juice (.25 tsp)
- ✓ Garlic powder (1 Tbsp.)
- ✓ Hoisin sauce (1 Tbsp.)
- ✓ Sweet chili sauce (.25 c.)
- ✓ Peeled and diced mangos (2)
- ✓ Lettuce leaves (6)
- ✓ Coconut oil (1 Tbsp.)
- ✓ Tempeh (16 oz.)

Directions:
1. Take out a big skillet and heat up some of the coconut oil on top. Cook the tempeh until it starts to crumble and is browned, making sure to stir it the whole time.
2. After about four minutes of cooking this, add in the salt, garlic, lime juice, and hoisin and heat it all the way through.
3. Slice up the mangoes into smaller cubes and then pour the sweet chili sauce into a bowl to mix with the cubes.
4. Scoop up your cooked tempeh and divide it up between lettuce's leaves to use those as your wraps. Top with some of the mango chunks and then serve.

***

Creamy Squash Pizza

Ingredients:

Sauce
- ✓ Oregano (1 tsp.)
- ✓ Paprika (1 tsp.)
- ✓ Cumin (1 tsp.)
- ✓ Red pepper flakes (1 tsp.)
- ✓ Olive oil (1 Tbsp.)
- ✓ Minced garlic (2 Tbsp.)
- ✓ Cubed butternut squash (3 c.)

Crust
- ✓ Onion powder (1 tsp.)
- ✓ Italian seasoning (1 Tbsp.)
- ✓ Minced garlic (2 Tbsp.)
- ✓ Water (2 c.)
- ✓ French green lentils (2 c.)

Toppings
- ✓ Olive oil (1 Tbsp.)
- ✓ Diced purple onion (1)
- ✓ Diced head of broccoli (1)
- ✓ Diced red bell pepper (1)
- ✓ Diced green bell pepper (1)

Directions:
1. Turn on the oven and give it some time to heat up to 350 degrees. While the oven is heating up, use your favorite method to heat up the French green lentils.
2. When you are ready, add all of the ingredients for the sauce into a food processor or blender and then blend on a low setting until all of this is mixed and the sauce starts to look creamy. Set this aside in a small bowl for now.
3. Clean out the food processor, and then add the ingredients you are using for your crust. Pulse this at high speed to make a batter that is like dough.
4. Heat up a deep-dish pan over your stove and grease it with just a bit of oil. Press this dough into the skillet to make it into a round pizza. When that is done, add to the oven to bake.
5. After a few minutes, about five, you can put the crust onto a baking tray with some parchment paper and then top with the sauce and the rest of the toppings. Add to the oven to bake.
6. This needs to cook for around 15 minutes. When that time is up, take this out of the oven and slice up into four parts before serving.

***

Portobello Burgers

Ingredients:
- ✓ Salt
- ✓ Chili powder (.5 tsp.)
- ✓ Paprika (.5 tsp.)
- ✓ Taco seasoning (1 Tbsp.)
- ✓ Drained tofu (8 oz.)
- ✓ Olive oil (1 Tbsp.)
- ✓ Salsa (.25 c.)
- ✓ Vegan buns (2)
- ✓ Hummus (4 Tbsp.)
- ✓ Red and green bell pepper, diced (.5 each)
- ✓ Onion diced (.5)
- ✓ Mushroom caps, portobello (4)
- ✓ Spinach (3 c.)

Directions:
1. Take the tofu and slice it up into four pieces. Then you can take out the skillet and warm up with some of the olive oil.
2. When this is warm, add in the mushrooms caps and then let them cook for four minutes before slipping them over. Sprinkle on the chili powder, taco seasoning, salt, and paprika.
3. Flip these again after another four minutes and then leave them to cook until they are about half their original size. When this is done, take them off the heat and set to the side.
4. Add your prepared slices of tofu and cook on both sides to make browned a bit and hen set to the side.
5. Now it is time to add both the peppers and the onion to the skillet. These need to cook for about 10 minutes so the vegetables can become brown.
6. When this happens, you can turn the heat down to a low setting and put the mushrooms back in to heat up.
7. While those are cooking, you can spread out the hummus on one side of your bun and then add the salsa to the other part. Top the hummus with a bit of spinach.
8. Serve this with two of the tofu squares and two of the mushrooms, and as much of the vegetables as you would like and enjoy.

Sweet and Sour Tofu

Ingredients:
- ✓ Drained tofu (14 oz)
- ✓ Olive oil (2 Tbsp.)
- ✓ Chopped red bell pepper (1)
- ✓ Coconut sugar (1 Tbsp.)
- ✓ Cornstarch (1 tsp.)
- ✓ Minced garlic (.2 Tbsp>)
- ✓ Diced white onion (1)
- ✓ Minced ginger (.5-inch piece)
- ✓ Cornstarch (1 tsp)
- ✓ Soy sauce (2 Tbsp.)
- ✓ Rice vinegar (2 Tbsp.)
- ✓ Pineapple chunks (1 c.)
- ✓ Tomato paste (1 Tbsp.)
- ✓ Chopped green and red bell pepper (1 of each)

Directions:
1. Take out a small bowl and then whisk together the sugar, cornstarch, vinegar, tomato paste, and soy sauce.
2. Slice up the tofu into cubes and add into a bowl with the soy sauce mixture. Let this set to marinate the tofu for some time.
3. After the marinating is done, heat up a bit of the oil in a frying pan and when this is warm, add in the chunks of tofu and half of the marinade that is left into the pan. Let this cook.
4. After about 10 minutes, with lots of stirring in the process, you can take the tofu off the heat and let it set in a bowl.
5. Add the rest of the oil to the same pan and then put the garlic and ginger inside. Heat this up for a minute before adding in the peppers and onion. Cook these to help the vegetables get nice and soft.
6. After another 5 minutes, you can pour the rest of the marinade into the pan with the vegetables and let these heat up until the sauce can get thick.
7. Add in the tofu cubes and the pineapple chunks and cook to heat up before serving.

BBQ Sliders

Ingredients:

- ✓ Tomatoes, pickles, onions for topping
- ✓ Asian style slaw for topping
- ✓ Slider buns (6)
- ✓ Onion powder (1 tsp.)
- ✓ Garlic powder (1 tsp.)
- ✓ BBQ sauce (.5 c.)
- ✓ Green jackfruit (2 cans)

Directions:

1. Bring out a big bowl and use a fork or your own potato masher to help get the jackfruit mashed to a shredded type of consistency.
2. Heat up a stockpot and add in the onion powder, garlic powder, BBQ sauce, and shredded jackfruit.
3. Stir this around and cover the pot. After 10 minutes, then you can take the lid off.
4. If you notice that the jackfruit is starting to stick then you can add in a bit of water or vegetable broth to help with this.
5. When the lid is off, you can cook for a few more minutes to heat all the way up.
6. Serve this on some of the slider buns and add on your favorite toppings before serving.

Hawaiian Burgers

Ingredients:

- ✓ Toppings of your choice
- ✓ Buns (8)
- ✓ Pineapple sliced into rings (1)
- ✓ Onion powder (1 tsp.)
- ✓ Garlic powder (1 tsp.)
- ✓ Pineapple juice (.25 c.)
- ✓ BBQ sauce (.25 c.)
- ✓ Quick-cooking oats (1 .c)
- ✓ Cooked brown rice (2 c.)
- ✓ Cooked black beans (3 c.)

Directions:

1. Turn on the grill at the beginning of this and get it up to medium-high heat.
2. In the meantime, take out a bowl and use a fork to help mash the black beans in. then add in the onion powder, garlic powder, pineapple juice, BBQ sauce, oats, and rice into it.
3. Combine this mixture until it can hold its own shape and can be formed into patties.
4. Scoop out about half a cup of this and form into a patty. Repeat to use up the whole mixture and then add these onto the grill.
5. Cook for about 5 minutes on one side and then flip them over to cook on that side.
6. Add the pineapple rings to the grill at this time and only cook for a few minutes on each side.
7. When this is done, take the pineapple rings and burgers off the grill. Add one pineapple ring and one patty onto each bun.
8. Top with some of the BBQ sauce and some of the favorite toppings you chose before serving.

***

Falafel Burgers

Ingredients:

- ✓ Favorite toppings
- ✓ Whole-wheat buns or pita pockets
- ✓ Ground pepper (.25 tsp.)
- ✓ Ground coriander (1 tsp.)
- ✓ Ground cumin (1.5 tsp.)
- ✓ Onion powder (2 tsp.)
- ✓ Garlic powder (2 tsp.)
- ✓ Lemon juice (1 Tbsp.)
- ✓ Chopped parsley that is fresh (.25 c.)
- ✓ Vegetable broth (.25 c.)
- ✓ Brown rice that is cooked (2 c.)
- ✓ Cooked chickpeas (3 c.)

Directions:

1. Turn on the oven and let it heat up to 425 degrees. While the oven is heating up, you can take out a baking sheet and line it with some parchment paper.
2. Now bring out your food processor and combine the pepper, coriander, onion powder, cumin, garlic powder, lemon juice, parsley, broth, rice, and chickpeas.
3. Process these ingredients together for about half a minute. You don't want it to turn into hummus but have it enough so that it forms into patties.
4. When this is done take about half a cup of the mixture and form it into patties. Add onto your prepared baking sheet, and then repeat that with the rest of the mixture.
5. Add this to the oven and let it bake. After 15 minutes, take these out of the oven and then flip them around before cooking for another 15 minutes.
6. When this is done, take the patties out of the oven to cool down. Fill up the buns or the pitas with some of your favorite toppings, and then add in the burgers to serve.

Black Bean and Quinoa Burgers

Ingredients:

- ✓ Roasted sesame seeds
- ✓ Lettuce leaves (4)
- ✓ Pepper (1 tsp.)
- ✓ Salt (1 tsp.)
- ✓ Dry black beans (1 .c)
- ✓ Dry quinoa (.5 c.)
- ✓ Chopped purple onion (.5)
- ✓ Paprika (.5 tsp.)
- ✓ Olive oil (2 Tbsp.)
- ✓ Red pepper flakes (.5 tsp.)
- ✓ Minced garlic (2 Tbsp.)
- ✓ Whole wheat flour (.5 c.)
- ✓ Chopped bell pepper (.25 c.)

Directions:

1. Start out this recipe by preparing the beans using your favorite method. You can also take this time to prepare the quinoa-based on the instructions on the back of the box.
2. When you are ready, heat up a bit of olive oil in a frying pan and when it is nice and hot, add in the onions, bell peppers, and garlic and then season with some pepper and salt.
3. Cook these until you are able to get the vegetables to soften, which can take around five minutes. When that time is done, take the pan from the heat and let them cool down.
4. When these are all cooled down, which can take around 10 minutes, you can add the vegetables to the food processor along with the rest of the spices, the quinoa, flour, and cooked beans. Pulse to make this into a chunky mixture.
5. Take out a pan and cover it with some parchment paper. Form this mixture into four patties and then add to the freezer for the next five minutes to help them stick together better.
6. When that time is up, add the rest of the oil to a frying pan and heat it up. When the pan is warm, add the patties inside.
7. Cook these until all of the sides are browned, which will take about 3 minutes on aside. Serve these with a burger bun or lettuce leaf and some of your favorite toppings.

***

Stuffed Peppers

Ingredients:
- ✓ Pepper
- ✓ Salt
- ✓ Dry black beans (1 c.)
- ✓ Dry chickpeas (.5 c.)
- ✓ Kale (.5 c)
- ✓ Parsley (1 Tbs.)
- ✓ Water (2 Tbsp.)
- ✓ Olive oil (2 Tbsp.)
- ✓ Bell peppers, any color (3)
- ✓ Dry quinoa (.5 co
- ✓ Sweet onion, chopped (1)
- ✓ Garlic, minced (2 Tbsp.)

Directions:
1. Start out by preparing the beans by following your favorite method. You can also go through and prepare the quinoa using the directions that are on the package.
2. In the meantime, you can heat up the oven and let it get to 400 degrees. While that is heating up, you can slice up the bell peppers and get rid of the stem and the seeds.
3. Add these to the baking sheet, make sure to have the skin down, and add a bit of the oil. Add to the oven
4. After about 10 minutes, the skin on the peppers should be softening and it is time to take them out and let them cool down.
5. While your peppers are in the oven add some oil to a pan and heat it up. Add in the onion and let it cook for a few minutes before stirring in the water, parsley, kale, garlic, and basil.
6. Cook all of these together for a few more minutes before adding in the prepared chickpeas, quinoa, and black beans, warming them all the way through.
7. Spoon this mixture into the cooked pepper halves and then put all of this back into the oven to heat up.
8. After another 10 minutes, you can take the bell peppers out of the oven and let them cool down before serving.

Sweet Potato Sushi

Ingredients:

- ✓ Tamari (1 Tbsp)
- ✓ Silken tofu (14 oz.)
- ✓ Nori sheets (4)
- ✓ Agave nectar (1 Tbsp.)
- ✓ Rice vinegar (1 Tbsp.)
- ✓ Dry sushi rice (.75 c)
- ✓ Peeled sweet potato (1)
- ✓ Sliced avocado (1)
- ✓ Water (1 c)

Directions:

1. Turn on the oven and give it time to heat up to 400 degrees. While that is warming up, take the tamari and mix it together with the agave nectar until they are combined together well and then set to the side.
2. Next, we need to slice up the sweet potato into sticks and place them onto a prepared baking sheet. Coat them with some of the agave and tamari mixtures. Add to the oven.
3. Bake these in the oven until they get nice and soft, making sure to flip them around during the cooking process as well.
4. After 25 minutes, these will be done. In the meantime, bring out a pot and add the vinegar, water, and the sushi rice inside. Bring this to a boil and let it cook until most of the liquid is gone, which will take around ten minutes.
5. While we are cooking the rice, we can cut up the tofu into long sticks and set it aside. Take the pot off the heat when they are done and let the rice sit for about 10 minutes.
6. Cover up the work surface that you are using with some parchment paper and wet your fingers. Layout the nori sheet on here and add a thin layer of the rice. Leave some room to roll up the sheet.
7. Add the strips of roasted sweet potato on here in a straight line, and then lay the avocado and tofu slices right beside them as well.
8. When this is done, you can roll up the nori sheet into a tight cylinder. Slice this into 8 pieces and then put it in the fridge. Repeat with the rest of the nori sheets and fillings.
9. Serve this chilled and enjoy.

Sweet Potato Chili

Ingredients:

- ✓ Chopped parsley
- ✓ Pepper
- ✓ Salt
- ✓ Olive oil (1 Tbsp.)
- ✓ Water (.5 c)
- ✓ Cayenne (.5 tsp.)
- ✓ Paprika (.5 tsp.)
- ✓ Chili powder (1 Tbsp.)
- ✓ Red bell pepper (.5)
- ✓ Cumin (1 tsp.)
- ✓ Green bell pepper (.5)
- ✓ Tofu, (14 oz.)
- ✓ Diced tomatoes with green chilies (1 can)
- ✓ Sweet potatoes, cubed (2)
- ✓ Diced onion, sweet (1)

Directions:

1. To start this recipe, take out a pot and heat up some of the olive oil inside. When that is warm, add in the garlic and onions and let them cook until they are nice and soft.
2. When this is done, add in the bell peppers and stir to make it all nice and tender, which can take another five minutes.
3. When five minutes is up, you can reduce the heat to low and add in your remaining ingredients. Stir this around to combine well and let it cook.
4. After another 20 minutes, the sweet potatoes should be soft, and the liquid should be nice and thick.
5. Serve this in a warm bowl and enjoy!

***

Coconut Tofu Curry

Ingredients:

- ✓ Pepper
- ✓ Salt
- ✓ Firm tofu (14 oz.)
- ✓ Agave nectar (1 tsp.)
- ✓ Coconut oil (2 tsp.)
- ✓ Red pepper flakes (.5 tsp.)
- ✓ Can of coconut milk (13 oz.)
- ✓ Cumin (1 tsp.)
- ✓ Diced tomatoes (1)
- ✓ Curry powder (1 tsp.)
- ✓ Turmeric (1 tsp.)
- ✓ Snap peas (1 c.)
- ✓ Ginger, minced

Directions:

1. To start this recipe, slice the tofu into smaller cubes. Then take out a skillet and heat up the coconut oil inside to make it hot.
2. When the oil is nice and warm, add in the tofu and let it cook for a bit. After 5 minutes, add in the onion and garlic and cook for another five minutes before adding in the ginger as well.
3. When that is nice and warmed up, it is time to add in the rest of the spices along with the snap peas, tomatoes, coconut milk, and agave nectar.
4. Combine well and then cover up the pot cooking this on low heat. After another 10 minutes, you can take the whole pot off the heat.
5. When you are ready to serve, scoop this prepared curry onto some rice or into a bowl and enjoy it.

***

Tahini Falafels

Ingredients:

- ✓ Tahini (2 Tbsp.)
- ✓ Salt
- ✓ Turmeric (.25 tsp.)
- ✓ Paprika (.5 tsp.)
- ✓ Lemon juice (.5 tsp.)
- ✓ Olive oil (1 tsp.)
- ✓ Cumin (2 tsp.)
- ✓ Minced garlic clove (1)
- ✓ Broccoli florets (2 c.)
- ✓ Black beans dry (.5 c.)
- ✓ Dry chickpeas (2 c.)

Directions:

1. You can cook up the black beans and the chickpeas by following the method you want to use.
2. While those are cooking, you can turn on the oven to 400 degrees and let it get warm.
3. Take out a skillet and drizzle some broccoli florets with the oil and salt. Add the broccoli to the warm skillet and let them cook to become brown and tender. This should be done after ten minutes.
4. When that is done, move the broccoli off the heat and let it cool down. Add this prepared broccoli into the food processor with all of your ingredients besides the tahini and blend until it is smooth and most of the lumps are gone.
5. Take out a baking pan and add some parchment paper to it. Press the dough that you just made into 8 patties that are equal, and then place them on the parchment paper. Add to the oven.
6. Bake these until they are crisp and brown on the outside, which can take around 15 minutes. Make sure that you flip these around about halfway through so that the cooking is even as possible.
7. Serve with the tahini as a topping and enjoy.

Baked Enchilada

Ingredients:

- ✓ Vegan cheese (.5 c.)
- ✓ Salt (1 tsp.)
- ✓ Garlic powder (1 tsp)
- ✓ Paprika (1 tsp.)
- ✓ Chopped cashews (.5 c.)
- ✓ Cumin (1 tsp.)
- ✓ Firm tofu (14 oz.)
- ✓ Diced purple onion (.5)
- ✓ Green pepper (1)
- ✓ Enchilada sauce (2 c.)
- ✓ Olive oil (4 Tbsp.)
- ✓ Sweet potato (1)
- ✓ Black beans (1 c.)
- ✓ Chopped jalapenos (1 Tbsp.)

Directions:

1. Turn on the oven and let it heat up to 400 degrees. While that is warming up, take the sweet potatoes and slice them into cubes before adding them to a big bowl.
2. Top with a bit of olive oil, salt, and garlic powder. Toss these around so that the sweet potatoes will be coated as evenly as possible.
3. When this is done, add to the prepared baking pan and then put them in the oven to cook until they are soft. This will take around 20 minutes.
4. While those are baking, dice up the tofu onion, and bell pepper into small cubes and then place into the bowl with the salt, cashews, and olive oil. Stir these well to make sure it is all coated evenly.
5. When the potatoes are done, add the onion, peppers, and tofu to the baking pan and then stir to combine. Add all of these back into the oven to bake for a bit.
6. After ten minutes, the peppers should be soft and the onions brown. Take these out of the oven and then place it into a casserole dish.
7. Add the black beans, spices, and the enchilada sauce to the dish and mix to make sure it is all combined. Top with your vegan cheese before adding back into the oven to bake.
8. After another 15 minutes, this should be done. Take it out of the oven and give it some time to cool down. Top with the jalapenos and then serve.

Energy Crackers

Ingredients:

- ✓ Pepper
- ✓ Salt
- ✓ Flax seeds (.25 c.)
- ✓ Chia seeds (.25 c.)
- ✓ Paprika powder (.25 tsp.)
- ✓ Sesame seeds (.25 c)
- ✓ Water (.75 c.)
- ✓ Minced garlic (1 Tbsp.)
- ✓ Cashews crushed (.25 c.)
- ✓ Crushed peanuts (.25 c.)
- ✓ Dried onion flakes (.5 Tbsp.)
- ✓ Pumpkin seeds (.5 c)

Directions:
1. To start this recipe, turn on the oven and let it heat up to 350 degrees. While the oven is heating up, take out a big bowl and combine the onion flakes, water, garlic, and paprika. Mix together well.
2. You will want to add the chia seeds, sesame seeds, pumpkin seeds, cashews, peanuts, and flax seeds to that same bowl.
3. Stir all of this together well but add in some pepper and salt to your own preferences here.
4. When that is done, take out a baking sheet and line it with some parchment paper. Spread out this mixture and then add it to the heated oven.
5. After 25 minutes, these should be done. Take them out of the oven and then flip it over so that it is easier to cut.
6. Slice into as many squares as you would like, and then put it back into the oven to finish baking.
7. After another half an hour, these crackers are done. Allow them to have some time cooling down before serving.

***

Chocolate and Zucchini Muffins

Ingredients:

- ✓ Water (.5 c.)
- ✓ Salt
- ✓ Nutmeg (.5 tsp.)
- ✓ Vanilla (.5 tsp.)
- ✓ Cinnamon (.5 tsp.)
- ✓ Baking powder (2 tsp.)
- ✓ Almond milk 5 Tbsp.)
- ✓ Dark chocolate chips (.5 c.)
- ✓ Chocolate protein powder (1 c.)
- ✓ Shredded zucchini (.5 c.)
- ✓ Maple syrup (.25 c.)
- ✓ Applesauce (.5 c.)
- ✓ Banana (2)
- ✓ Chopped walnuts (.5 c.)
- ✓ Almond flour (1.5 c.)
- ✓ Coconut oil (2 Tbsp.)
- ✓ Dry quinoa (.5 c.)

Directions:

1. Take the time to follow the directions on the back of the box to cook up and prepare the quinoa that we are using.
2. Turn on the oven and give it time to heat up to 400 degrees. While that is getting nice and warm, prepare a muffin pan with some coconut oil and set to the side.
3. Now we need to take out a big bowl and mix together the baking powder, cinnamon, walnuts, salt, nutmeg, flour, and prepared quinoa.
4. Then bring out a second bowl and mash together the bananas with a fork. Combine these with the applesauce.
5. Stir in the almond milk, protein powder, maple syrup, and vanilla until they are distributed well, adding in some more water if it is needed.
6. Combine these two separate mixtures into one bowl and then stir to make sure the batter is all smooth. Then finally fold in the chocolate chips and the shredded zucchini.
7. Take the batter and fill up the muffin cups to the halfway point. Then add these to the oven to bake.
8. After 20 minutes, you can take these out of the oven and let them cool down a bit before serving or storing.

***

Lemon Pie Bars

Ingredients:

- ✓ Salt (.25 tsp.)
- ✓ Lemon juice (2 Tbsp.)
- ✓ Protein powder, vanilla (.5 c.)
- ✓ Pitted dates (2 c.)
- ✓ Sunflower seeds (.33 c.)
- ✓ Raw cashews (.33 c.)
- ✓ Pecan pieces (.25 c.)
- ✓ Chia seeds (.25 c.)

Directions:

1. Take some time before we start to soak our chia seeds in some water. Drain out the water that is left when you are done.
2. Next, take out the food processor and then place the sunflower seeds, chia seeds, pecans, and cashews inside. Let these pulse on a low setting until you get a crumbly mixture out of them.
3. Now it is time to add the dates, lemon juice, and salt and then continue to pulse while you add in some of the protein powder so you get a chunky kind of dough.
4. Add this o a baking sheet that has some parchment paper on it. Press this out using a rolling pin to get a nice thick square.
5. Add this to the freezer to get it to set, for about 60 minutes. When the chunk is solid you can slice into 8 pieces and enjoy.

***

Spicy Chickpea Poppers

Ingredients:

- ✓ Cayenne pepper (.25 tsp.)
- ✓ Paprika (.25 tsp.)
- ✓ Cumin (.25 tsp.)
- ✓ Onion powder (.25 tsp.)
- ✓ Garlic powder (.5 tsp.)
- ✓ Chili powder (.5 tsp.)
- ✓ Salt (.5 tsp.)
- ✓ Coconut oil (1 Tbsp.)
- ✓ Chickpeas (2 c.)

Directions:

1. Take some time to cook the chickpeas according to the method that you like the most.
2. When those are done, you can turn on the oven and let it heat up to 400 degrees. While the oven is getting warm, use some parchment paper to line the baking sheet.
3. Add the chickpeas when they are done to a big plate, and then pat them dry. Add to the baking sheet before coating with the garlic powder, onion powder, salt, and coconut oil.
4. Add these to the oven so the chickpeas can bake. When they are fragrant and brown, which will take around half an hour, then you can take them out of the oven.
5. Allow the chickpeas some time to cool down and then add them to a bowl. Mix with the rest of the spices that we have not used yet until coated well and then serve warm.

***

Almond Protein Bars

Ingredients:

- ✓ Coconut oil (1 tsp.)
- ✓ Applesauce (2 Tbsp.)
- ✓ Flax seeds (.25 c.)
- ✓ Chopped almonds (.25 c)
- ✓ Dried cranberries (.25 c.)
- ✓ Pitted dates (.5 c.)
- ✓ Chocolate protein powder (.5 c.)
- ✓ Almond butter (1 c)

Directions:

1. Take out a baking dish and line it with some parchment paper before setting it to the side.
2. Add all of your ingredients into the setup the food processor and then blend them together to make a thick dough.
3. Press this prepared dough into your baking dish, making sure here to properly press it into each corner. You can use your hands to make sure this is pressed down as well as possible throughout the whole pan.
4. Add this to the fridge to set for about two hours. If you need it done a bit faster, add to the freezer and chill for an hour.
5. Slice into 8 bars and then enjoy or serve right away.

Matcha Energy Balls

Ingredients:

- ✓ Maple syrup (1 Tbsp.)
- ✓ Matcha powder (1 Tbsp.)
- ✓ Raw cashews (1 c.)
- ✓ Pistachios (.5 c.)
- ✓ Crushed hazelnuts (.25 c.)
- ✓ Coconut, shredded (.25 c.)
- ✓ Vanilla protein powder (.5 c.)
- ✓ Packed and pitted dates (.5 c.)

Directions:

1. Bring out a food processor and get it all set up nicely. Add in all of the ingredients outside of the hazelnuts to the food processor and then blend on low to combine and crush well.
2. When this is done, bring out a spoon and scoop out heaps of this mixture. Use your own hands along the way in order to roll into balls.
3. After they are crushed, pour the hazelnuts into a bowl and then roll the matcha balls into the hazelnuts until they are coated all around.
4. Add these, when they are all coated, into the fridge and let them sit there until they are solid. This will take about half an hour to finish and then serve!

***

Black Bean Dip

Ingredients:

- ✓ Salt (.25 tsp.)
- ✓ Lemon juice (1 Tbsp.)
- ✓ Olive oil (1 Tbsp.)
- ✓ Onion powder (2 Tbsp.)
- ✓ Italian seasoning (2 Tbsp.)
- ✓ Minced garlic (2 Tbsp.)
- ✓ Cooked black beans (4 c.)

Directions:

1. Take all of the black beans and add them into a bowl. Mash these up with a fork until you get them to be pretty smooth.
2. When this is done, you can stir in the rest of the ingredients and incorporate them well. You want to make sure this mixture is as creamy and smooth as possible.
3. Add in some more lemon juice and salt to taste if you would like, and then serve at room temperature.

Sunflower Protein Bars

Ingredients:

- ✓ Salt (.25 tsp.)
- ✓ Nutmeg (.25 tsp.)
- ✓ Cinnamon (1 tsp.)
- ✓ Vanilla (2 tsp.)
- ✓ Sunflower butter (.5 c.)
- ✓ Maple syrup (.5 c)
- ✓ Chocolate protein powder (1 c.)
- ✓ Rice cereal puffy (1 c.)
- ✓ Old fashioned oats (1 c.)

Directions:

1. Take out a big bowl and mix together the salt, nutmeg, cinnamon, protein powder, rice cereal, and oats. Set this to the side.
2. In a second bowl, you are able to add in the maple syrup and the sunflower butter and heat it up in the microwave for about half a minute.
3. When this is done, take it out of the microwave and then add it to the bowl with the dry ingredients. Stir these together well until you have a mixture that is smooth and no lumps are present.
4. Spread this mixture out into a shallow dish that has some parchment paper and then pack it down inside firmly. Use a spoon if needed to help get rid of the air bubbles.
5. Move this dish to the freezer and then let it set in there for about 20 minutes. When this is done, take the dish back out and slice into 6 parts before enjoying it.

***

Cake Batter Smoothie

Ingredients:

- ✓ Nutmeg (.25 tsp.)
- ✓ Vanilla (1 tsp.)
- ✓ Cinnamon (1 tsp.)
- ✓ Cashew butter (1 Tbsp.)
- ✓ Chocolate protein powder (4 Tbsp.)
- ✓ Quick oats (.25 c.)
- ✓ Almond milk (1 c.)
- ✓ Banana (1)

Directions:

1. Bring out a small jar or bowl and mix together the almond milk and your oats.
2. Add this into the fridge to give the oats some time to soften. Usually, this will need around an hour to complete.
3. After this time, add the milk and oats mixture into the blender with the rest of the ingredients.
4. Blend this on high speed until you have it all smooth and the lumps are all gone. Serve in some tall glasses with a bit of cinnamon on top and enjoy.

***

Protein Trail Mix Bars

Ingredients:
- ✓ Salt (.25 tsp.)
- ✓ Cinnamon (.25 tsp.)
- ✓ Chocolate protein powder (.5 c.)
- ✓ Maple syrup (.25 c.)
- ✓ Raw walnuts (1 c.)
- ✓ Pecan halves (2 c.)
- ✓ Raw almonds (2 c.)

Directions:
1. Heat up a frying pan and when it is nice and warm, add in the protein powder, maple syrup, and nuts.
2. Stir this constantly so that the ingredients are going to turn into a thick and tacky kind of mixture. This can take up to ten minutes.
3. When that time is done, it is time to sprinkle on the cinnamon and salt over this and then cook for another few minutes.
4. When this is done, line a shallow pan with some parchment paper and then spread out the nut mixture onto it. Spread this out well and then give it some time to cool down all of the ways.
5. When you are ready to serve, you can go through and slice into 8 pieces before serving.

Mocha Chocolate Brownie Bars

Ingredients:

- ✓ Cold-brewed coffee (1 c)
- ✓ Agave nectar (2 Tbsp.)
- ✓ Nutmeg (.25 tsp.)
- ✓ Vanilla (1 tsp.)
- ✓ Quick oats (.5 c.)
- ✓ Cocoa powder (.5 c)
- ✓ Chocolate protein powder (2.5 c)

Directions:

1. Take out a baking dish and line it with a bit of parchment paper. Set it to the side.
2. When that is done, take out a bowl and mix together the dry ingredients. Slowly add in the cold coffee, vanilla, and agave nectar, making sure to stir the whole time so that the lumps in the mixture are going to disappear.
3. When you have gotten rid of all the lumps, pour this batter into your prepared dish, making sure to press it down in all of the corners.
4. Now it is time to add the dish to the fridge to set until firm. This can take about four hours, move it to the freezer, and sit for about an hour.
5. Slice this into 6 even squares and then serve.

Cherry Vanilla Protein Bars

Ingredients:

- ✓ Vanilla (1 Tbsp.)
- ✓ Almond milk (1 Tbsp.)
- ✓ Chia seeds (.25 c.)
- ✓ Maple syrup (.25 c)
- ✓ Dried cranberries (.5 c.)
- ✓ Cashew butter (.4 c)
- ✓ Shredded coconut (.33 c.)
- ✓ Vanilla protein powder (2 c.)
- ✓ Oats (1 c.)

Directions:

1. To start this recipe, take out a baking dish and line it with some parchment paper before setting it to the side.
2. When that is done, take out a blender and add in the coconut, protein powder, and oats inside. You will want to blend this until they are in a nice fine powder.
3. When this one is done, move it to a big bowl and then add in the rest of the ingredients that you are using. Mix well with a spoon until it is thoroughly combined.
4. Move this dough into a baking dish, and then press down with your hands until you are able to get it to be as even as possible.
5. Place this into the freezer so that it has time to get firm. This will take around an hour and a half.
6. When that time is done, take it out of the freezer and slice into 8 bars before serving.

***

Banana and Peanut Butter Cookies

Ingredients:

- ✓ Salt (1 pinch)
- ✓ Cocoa nibs (1 Tbsp.)
- ✓ Nutmeg (.25 tsp.)
- ✓ Cinnamon (.5 tsp.)
- ✓ Vanilla (1 Tbsp.)
- ✓ Ground flaxseed (1 Tbsp.)
- ✓ Baking powder (1 Tbsp.)
- ✓ Chocolate protein powder (.5 c.)
- ✓ Maple syrup (.25 c.)
- ✓ Chopped peanuts (.25 c)
- ✓ Chunky peanut butter (.5 c.)
- ✓ Banana (1)
- ✓ Dry chickpeas (1 c.)

Directions:

1. You can go through and prepare the chickpeas using the method you like the best.
2. When those are done, turn on the oven and let it heat up to 375 degrees. Then take out a baking pan and line it with a bit of parchment paper before setting it to the side.
3. Continue to add the cooked chickpeas and the other ingredients besides the cocoa nibs, to your food processor. Pulse these on a low setting until you see the mixture is getting nice and smooth.
4. When that is done, move it to a big bowl and then nicely stir in the cocoa nibs that you are using.
5. Now it is time to take a spoon and spoon the batter you made onto the baking pan. Press down on the batter a bit to get even baking. Add the pan to the oven to bake.
6. After about 8 to 10 minutes, the cookies should be done. Take them out of the oven to cool down before serving warm.

CONCLUSION

Thank you for making it through to the end of *Vegan Meal Prep for Beginners*. Let's hope it was informative and able to provide you with all of the tools you need to achieve your goals, whatever they may be.

The next step is to get started using the vegan diet plan. This is one of the best options that you are able to work with, and there are so many health benefits that you can get when you follow this diet, much more than you will find with any other diet plan out there. And when we are able to combine it together with some of the great tips and suggestions that come with meal prepping, you will find that it is easier than ever to get all of the nutrients and health that you are looking for along the way.

This guidebook took the time to look more into how we can work with meal planning to make the vegan diet to make things a whole lot easier in the process. When we can make the meal plan easier so that we can go on the vegan diet without a lot of problems, this guidebook will take a look at it, which can help you lose a lot of weight and so much more.

There are many benefits to following the vegan diet, and working with some meal planning and can make life so much easier overall. When you are ready to work with the vegan diet and meal planning together to make life easier, make sure to check out this guidebook to get started.

Finally, if you found this book useful in any way, a review on Amazon is always appreciated!

Plant-Based Nutrition and High-Protein Meals for Vegan Athletes and Bodybuilders

Introduction

Congratulations on purchasing *The Vegan Athlete,* and thank you for doing so.

The following chapters will discuss all of the different parts of the vegan diet that you need to know in order to be successful as an athlete. When we think about the traditional athlete, especially when we are talking about those who spend time weight lifting and doing other strenuous kinds of exercises, we think of a completely different diet plan. We assume that the vegan diet is going to lack a lot of the important nutrients and the other things that these athletes need. But as we will find in this guidebook, the vegan diet may be the perfect choice for these athletes if they want to fill up with the best foods while ensuring that they can get their best performance ever as well.

There are a lot of topics about the vegan diet for athletes, and we are going to take some time to explore as many of them as possible in this guidebook. We are going to start out with a little look at the vegan diet and what it is all about. We can talk about the basics, some of the rules for eating on this diet, and even a look at some of the health benefits and more of following this diet plan. The vegan diet, when it is done with whole and plant-based food and not with a bunch of junk that is labeled as vegan, can be one of the healthiest diet plans around, and we are going to take a look at how this is so.

When that is done, it is time for us to move on to some of the other things that we need to know when it comes to the vegan diet and using it for the athletes we know. We will take a look at how the protein found in our diets is so important and how the vegan diet can meet this, even for the bodybuilder and the athlete. Then we will have a discussion about anaerobic exercise and some of the unique nutritional requirements of these individuals, with a discussion of how the vegan diet will be able to meet those as well.

While the topics above are going to be very important, we are also going to take some time to explore how the vegan diet is going to be able to help us out as bodybuilders. We will look at how bodybuilders, in particular, are able to benefit from this kind of diet plan and some of the simple adjustments that we need to make to this diet plan to ensure that the bodybuilder is able to increase their performance, see the best results, and still get the healthy nutrition that they need.

When we are done taking a look at all of the great things about the vegan diet and why it is so amazing, it is time to dive into some of the delicious recipes that we are able to utilize here. There is so much to love about the vegan diet, and it is so important for us to see how tasty and delicious it can be, even for someone who is a beginner in using it and for someone who is an athlete. We will include a ton of recipes for breakfast, lunch, dinner, dessert, snacks, and more, and some of the nutritional information so you can make the best decisions for your meal planning needs.

As we can see, there are a ton of things to discuss when it comes to the vegan diet for athletes, and this guidebook is going to attempt to go through many of them so you can see that this is the best choice for you. When you are ready to get started on the vegan diet, and you want to see how this can work for your needs, make sure to check out this guidebook to help you get started.

There are plenty of books on this subject on the market, thanks again for choosing this one! Every effort was made to ensure it is full of as much useful information as possible. Please enjoy it!

PART 1
VEGAN DIET FOR ATHLETES

CHAPTER 1: WHAT IS THE VEGAN DIET?

No matter what your goals are, whether you are trying to crush your weight loss, you are trying to improve your heart health, cut down on blood pressure, or even fight off diabetes, you will need to choose a strong and effective diet plan to help you make this happen. And one of the healthiest and the most popular diet plans that are available for us to try now is known as the vegan diet.

When the vegan diet is done in the right manner, it is going to result in a lot of great health benefits. It can help the participant to get a lot more nutrients than they may be taking in with their traditional diet. It is going to help improve some of the control that the individual has on their blood sugar levels, and it can result in a trimmer waistline. You have to be careful not to go through and eat too many of the same foods, or you are going to run into trouble with nutrient deficiencies. But when you do it well, you will not run into issues at all.

Veganism will be a method of living that will try and exclude and take out all forms possible of animal exploitation and cruelty, whether for clothing, food, or any of the other purposes that are there. For these reasons and more, this kind of diet plan is going to be devoid of all animal products. This includes dairy, eggs, and meat.

There are a number of reasons why someone would choose to go on this kind of diet plan. The first reason is for their health. This is a great way to lose weight, improve your heart health, and so much more. Others are going to do it for environmental concerns, and some do it for ethics. There are a lot of reasons why people will choose to go on a diet plan like the vegan diet, and you can choose the reason that works the best for us.

Types of Vegan Diets

There are actually a few different versions of the vegan diet that someone is able to follow. Most of them can be healthy and good for your health, though a few are going to be a little bit questionable here, and you have to consider whether they are actually any better than the regular diet that you were on before. Some of the choices that you can make when it comes to the vegan diet will include:

1. **The whole-food vegan diet**. This is going to take some time to look at a lot of whole foods and have the participant eat mostly those. This is going to include lots of seeds, nuts, legumes, whole grains, and of course, a lot of fresh produce in order to get the nutrients that you need.

2. **The junk food vegan diet**. This is a version that you can go on, and you are sure to find a bunch of junk food that is technically vegan. But you will not lose a bit of weight because it is going to be full of fake and processed foods rather than the foods that are actually good for you and can help you to lose weight. You should stay away from this option as much as possible if you want to keep your health in line.

3. **Raw food vegan diet**. This is going to be the version of the diet that will still stick with a lot of healthy and whole foods but will require that we do not cook any of these at temperatures that are higher than 118 degrees at all.

4. **The thrive diet**. This is going to be one of the versions of the raw food vegan diet. Those who decide to follow this are going to eat a lot of whole foods that are based on plants that are going to be minimally cooked at some really low temperatures or that will be raw in the process.

5. **80/10/10**. With this diet plan, you are going to eat raw food vegan and limit your plants that are higher in fats, including nuts and sometimes avocados. This one can often be known as the fruitarian diet and will rely on soft greens and raw fruits instead.

6. **Raw until 4**. This is going to be a diet that is similar to what we talked about above, but it is going to change it up a bit and make it easier for some people to follow. With this one, you are going to consume a lot of raw foods until 4 in the afternoon. Then you have the option to cook up a meal that is based on plants for your dinner in the evening.

7. **The starch solution**. This one is going to focus a bit more on the cooked starches like rice and corn and potatoes and a bit less on the fruits that you want to eat.

Although there are going to be a lot of variations to the vegan diet that you are able to follow, you will find that they can all lead to a healthier method of eating than what you did in the past. This can be good news for those who are just getting started along the way. But keep in mind that most of the scientific research out there about this kind of diet plan will just focus n the vegan diet as a whole and hasn't been able to look at each of these on their own.

We have to remember that if we want to get all of the great benefits that are out there for the vegan diet, then we need to eat foods that are wholesome and good for us. There are a lot of fake products that are technically vegan, but they have been so processed and changed that they are not going to be good for us. If we make our vegan diet have just those foods, then we are technically vegan, but we are not getting the wholesome and good foods with all of the nutrients, and then we will not get the health benefits that we are looking for.

There are a lot of things to love when it comes to working with the vegan diet, and it is likely that you are going to fall in love with it in no time as well! It has all of the healthy ingredients that you need and so much more that will help you to feel good, gain the muscles that you want, and so much more!

The Health Benefits

In addition to helping athletes to get healthier and see some of the best results possible with the workouts they are doing, there are a lot of other health benefits that we are able to see along the way as well. The vegan diet is often seen as one of the healthiest diet plans out there for people to try, and there are a lot of benefits of going with this one compared to some of the others.

Because you are getting rid of a lot of the foods that are considered unhealthy, and because you are cutting out the bad fats, the sodium, and the processed foods and sugars, you are automatically helping your body to get all of the good nutrients that it is looking for rather than all of the bad.

Most of us can agree that the traditional American diet is not going to be all that healthy to follow. It may seem like a good idea to start, but it is going to be a mess on our bodies. It causes us to gain weight, can make it hard to keep our hearts nice and strong, and can cause a whole host of other problems in the process as well. It may taste good and be really convenient to follow, but it is not healthy, and it is making it hard to do well as an athlete.

This is why the vegan diet can be so healthy. We are replacing all of that bad stuff that we just talked about with some of the good and healthy foods that our bodies need in the process. You get to eat a lot of good whole grains, fruits and vegetables, and healthy fats that are going to be so amazing overall for helping you to look and feel your best overall. And because of this, you get the benefit of having some really healthy and good health benefits as well.

Those who have gone on the vegan diet, and eating the healthy version without all of the junk, have found that this is one of the best ways to lose weight, improve the health of the heart by lowering cholesterol and blood pressure, can help individuals to fight off issues with diabetes, and so much more in the process of following this kind of diet plan. It is as simple as that. You work to fill your body with lots of healthy foods and produce and things that are good for it, then it will learn how to heal and can do a much better job when it is time to perform in the manner that you would like.

Eating on the Vegan Diet

Before you are able to start out with any kind of diet plan, it is important for us to go through and be prepared with the right kind of eating plan here. We need to make sure that we are consuming the right foods and avoiding the wrong foods in the process. The easiest way to remember what you are not allowed to consume on the vegan diet is that you can't have any animal products at all.

What this means is that you need to keep out all of the meat and the poultry that was found in your regular diet. This would be the goose, turkey, chicken, beef pork, lamb ad so on. We also need to keep out all of the seafood and the fish, so anything that comes out of the sea needs to be avoided here as well. The meat part of this is pretty easy to understand and follow, so we don't need to spend a lot of time on this.

However, there are a few other groups of foods that need to be avoided when you are going with this kind of diet plan. Things like dairy, eggs, and beef products are all on the list of foods that need to be avoided. These come from animals, and so they are considered animal products. There are vegan kinds of milk and cheeses that you can use to replace these if needed, and there are other vegan-friendly eggs that you can make, so don't feel like you need to avoid these completely. There are other animal-based ingredients that you have to be careful about as well, including lactose, whey, and more.

Now that we have listed out a lot of the things that you have to avoid when you are going through the vegan diet in order to get the best results from it. This is going to make you feel like there is nothing you are allowed to eat at all, and like you are lost for what will work or not. The good news is that once you get over the idea that there are a few things that you can't eat on this diet plan, there is a lot of great-tasting and delicious foods that are completely allowed, and you will still have a ton of tasty and delicious meals to enjoy on a regular basis.

There are many foods that we are able to enjoy, including some seitan, tempeh, and tofu that will provide us with a lot of protein. Legumes are good for a bit of protein and can provide us with a lot of other nutrients along with nuts, nut kinds of butter, and seeds. As we mentioned before, there are calcium-fortified yogurts and milk that are not dairy-based, such as cashew yogurt, so we can still get that vitamin B12 and D and the calcium for as long as we need.

Some of the other things that we are able to enjoy and eat plenty of when we are on the vegan diet will include things like nutritional yeast, whole grains, and other products that are made out of the whole grains, fermented and sprouted plant foods, and of course, lots of vegetables and fruits along the way as well.

Are There Risks?

There are a few risks with this diet plan when it comes to nutritional deficiencies along the way. Sometimes when we are changing over to this kind of diet plan and working on getting it all right and ensuring that we eat the right amounts and the right types of foods, deficiencies are going to show up on occasion. The good news, though, is if you do some meal planning and add a lot of variety to your meals, and you stick with the healthy foods and not all of the junk, even this is not going to be a problem. It may take a bit of trial and error to ensure that you can eat the right foods at the right times, but it evens out.

If you are worried about nutritional deficiencies when you first get started, then the best option is to start taking a multivitamin. This will be perfect for ensuring that you can get a lot of the important nutrients in as you make the adjustments. As you get more used to the vegan diet, this will not be as big of a problem, and you can stop taking the multivitamin if you would like and just focus on healthy and wholesome foods instead.

There are a lot of great things to love when it comes to working with a vegan diet. It is a simple diet plan that allows us to eat wholesome and good foods instead of eating all of the trash that is usually found on the traditional American diet. Following this kind of diet plan can help increase our performance, make it easier to lose weight, and be good for so many other health aspects. When you want a diet plan that is able to do it all, then the vegan diet is the right one to go with.

CHAPTER 2: WHY DOES PROTEIN MATTER?

When it comes to your athletic performance, there are a lot of different options and macronutrients that you need to consider. These are going to be so important to ensure that the body has all of the building blocks that it needs to stay healthy and happy for the long-term and not get sick in the process either. But one of the macronutrients that we need to focus on, and seems to be a topic of a lot of discussions when it comes to the vegan diet, is protein.

High-protein diets are going to be a really great thing when it comes to being a bodybuilder and trying to keep up with all of your athletic events. It is pretty common to see those who are on a diet grabbing some protein bars to help them to feel full and satisfied, and it is common for bodybuilders to take in several protein-shakes to help them go.

There is a lot of power behind this nutrient, and it is pretty easy to see where some of the excitement of consuming this and getting enough is going to come from. Protein is going to be such an important component that is seen in pretty much all of the cells of the body. Your nails and hair are going to be made up mostly of protein. Your body is able to utilize this protein to build up and repair the tissues when it is needed. It is also possible to use this protein to make hormones, enzymes, and some of the other chemicals that are important in the body. Protein is going to be one of the building blocks of the blood, skin, cartilage, muscles, and bones.

Along with carbs and fat, protein is one of the macronutrients that the body needs. This means that our body actually needs a relatively large amount of it to function properly. Minerals and vitamins, which we need but in a much smaller amount, are going to be known as micronutrients. But unlike carbs and fat, the body is not going to hold onto and store protein, which means that we are not going to have a good reservoir around to draw on later if it is needed.

Many people assume that this means they need to eat protein all day long. But this is not the truth. We actually need less protein than we think, even though most of us can benefit from getting our protein from better food sources. We have all heard in the past that getting extra protein is able to build up more muscle. But the only way to build up the muscle that we want is through lots of exercises. Bodies need to have a modest amount of protein to go through and function well. The extra protein is not going to come in and give us extra strength.

There are a number of rules that we are able to follow in order to help us get the moderate amounts of protein that we need.

1. Teenage boys that are active are able to get the majority of protein that they need with three daily servings for a total of seven ounces.

2. Children between the ages of 2 to 6 and most women, along with some of the elderly, will get what they need when they have two daily servings for a total of five ounces.

3. And for active women, most men, teen girls, and older children, the guidelines are going to be closer to two daily servings to end up being six ounces.

So for most people, eating an eight-ounce steak is going to be enough to give you the protein that your body needs and more. You should find some better options here, though. Steak is going to include a lot of the unhealthy saturated fats as well, and it is not allowed on the vegan diet to start with.

However, it is still important to make sure that we are taking in enough protein on a regular basis to help us to stay strong and to build up muscles. We don't need to just eat protein all day long, but adding some more into our diet plan will help us out so much. Some of the most important functions that we are able to see when we add more protein into our bodies include:

1. Maintenance and growth: Your body needs to have a lot of protein to help tissues to grow and stay strong. Under normal circumstances, the body is going to break down the same amount of protein that it will use to repair and build up tissue. But then there will be times when the body will break down more protein than it is able to create, such as while pregnant and when sick. Taking in more protein during this time can be important.

2. Can cause some biochemical reactions: Enzymes are going to be some proteins that will help to aid in all of the biochemical reactions that will take place in and out of your cells. These can help out with a lot of different things, including the contractions of muscles, blood clotting, energy protection, and digestion.

3. It can be a messenger: It is possible for proteins to become hormones so that they are the chemical messengers that will aid in the communication between the organs, tissues, and cells. They are going to be made and then secreted through the glands and endocrine tissues, and then your blood can move them around to reach their goal and send the message.

4. It can provide structure. Some of the proteins that you are able to work with are fibrous and can provide our tissues and cells with stiffness and the rigidity that it needs. Some of the proteins that we want to work with here include elastin, collagen, and keratin, which can help

us to form some of the connective frameworks of certain structures in the body.

5. It can help to bolster the immune systems. Proteins will help us form some immunoglobulins, which are known as antibodies, to fight infections. Antibodies are just going to be proteins that go to your blood to help make sure that your body is protected against viruses and bacteria. The more protein you have in your body and the more it is used well, the less likely you are to get sick.

6. It can help to transport and store all of the nutrients you need. This can include a lot of nutrients like oxygen, cholesterol, blood sugar, and various minerals and vitamins. Protein transporters are going to be really specific, which means that they are just going to bind to some specific substances and nothing else.

7. It can provide us with more energy: It is possible that protein will help us get energy and keep on moving during our workouts. But we do have to remember that our body's last thing that will use up for energy is protein because it is a valuable nutrient and so many parts of the body use it. This is why we usually rely on fats and carbs to keep us going.

As we can already guess, there are a lot of benefits of working with protein, and a bodybuilder or athlete will be able to enjoy a lot of them along the way. Utilizing the protein and getting enough on the vegan diet is usually easier than it may seem, as long as we plan out our meals well and don't eat a lot of junk in the process. Even without animal products, there are options that will allow us to get the protein that we need, which can be great news.

Chapter 3: How to Get the Right Nutrition for Anaerobic Activity

When you are a bodybuilder, it is important to go through and make sure that you are eating a healthy diet the whole time. This will ensure that you can get all of the nutrition that you need and make it a lot easier for you to stay healthy and happy over the long-term. Getting the right nutrition for this kind of activity is a bit of a challenge, and sometimes you will find that some of the other diet plans are not going to meet the nutrition values as you would like. But we will take some time in this chapter to look at the best ways to follow the vegan diet and provide our bodies with the right nutrition for anaerobic activity.

You will find that your body can reach an anaerobic state when you can work at the near-maximum effort. This means doing something like sprinting as fast you can for 400 meters or doing a short set of repetitions with a real heavyweight. You cannot sustain this kind of state for a long time, so a workout that is anaerobic is going to include a series of lifts or sprints with minimal recovery that happens between them. When you do this, your body is able to convert the carbs that are present into quick energy, which is why they should be one of the main focuses when you plan the meal you want to eat before these workouts.

Carbs

This is why we need to focus on carbs. Unlike during some of the slower and more moderate exercises that you want to do, where your body can convert some of the stored fat into fuel, these workouts will require a really fast source of fuel to get it done. The glycogen stored in your liver and your muscles, which will be there mainly from the carbs that you eat before the workout, will be easy to digest and can provide us with the fuel that we need.

Think back to the vegan diet and some of the amazing parts that will show up with it. There are many benefits of choosing this kind of diet plan, and the best part is that there are a ton f healthy carbs that you can eat, including whole grains and all of that healthy produce along the way. This means that you are more likely to get the carbs that you need to do these anaerobic exercises in no time when you are on the vegan diet.

During some of the shorter bursts of the high-intensity work, your body is able to convert some of the glycogen that is stored and some of the carbs that were recently consumed and then turn it into ATP and into creatine phosphate. This combination is going to provide us with the system for fuel for all activities.

With this in mind, we have to remember that it is important to stay away from some things like protein, fat, and fiber right before the workout. These are great additions to have in your diet during the rest of the day, but shortly before we go through one of the anaerobic exercises that we want to use, we need to make sure that we are avoiding these and keeping them out of our meals as much as possible.

Although whole grains are amazing and are going to provide us with a lot of nutritional benefits, they will contain a lot of fiber, which is going to slow down how quickly the carbs can go through the digestion process. If you take on too much fiber in the few hours before this kind of workout, you may not end up with the access that you need to that fuel source, and it could end up with a lot of digestive distress in the process.

When you are creating your own pre-workout meal, you need to stick with some of the carbs that are a bit easier to digest and eat up. This would be the white bread and the sugars. You are having too much protein and fat before the workout can cause a similar kind of effect on the body when it comes to your digestion and energy levels because your body needs to go through a complex process before turning these nutrients into fuel. A little protein and fat in the meal before a workout are fine, but you do need to keep it to a minimum rather than letting it be the main event all of the time.

While we are on the subject, we need to talk about your meal's timing before the workout. If you have a meal that falls three to four hours before you plan to exercise, you are able to have a full meal that will have around 300 to 500 calories on it. Some of the things you may want to try out here include a bagel, a nice salad with some tempeh or seitan on it, or a potato with some cashew yogurt or salsa on it.

If you are only an hour or two from the workout, we need to shrink the portion size a bit to not still digest it all. You could go with a cup of cashew yogurt, a fruit smoothie, or even a piece of fruit to get the energy that you need. And if your workout is even closer, say within half an hour, then going with a sports gel, a sports drink, or an apple can be what you need to get the carbs and the energy that you need to finish up this kind of workout.

Unlike some of the athletes out there who work more on endurance, the anaerobic athletes will not really need to focus on carb-loading at all. This idea of carb loading is going to involve eating a higher percentage, sometimes as high as 70 to 75 percent of our daily calories, from carbs for a few days before a competition or a big workout. The reason that some athletes will do this is to help them maximize the stores of energy that are found in their muscles.

This is not something that really needs to be done in an anaerobic workout. These are going to utilize some of the glycogen that is stored in the muscles, but it is unlikely that you are going to go through and deplete the stores so much that you won't have any let because the workouts are going to be so small and will not last all that long.

Anaerobic exercise is going to work in a slightly different manner than what we can find. We need to eat differently from we would with some of the other forms of working out and exercising that you may have heard about in the past. Knowing the best ways to eat and being prepared for this will ensure that we can take care of our bodies and eat the right foods at the right times, and the vegan diet can step in and help make this work out great.

Chapter 4: Why Bodybuilders Should Consider the Vegan Diet

When we hear about the vegan diet and the word bodybuilding, we are going to be a bit confused. It is not often that the two of these will come together and be used in the same sentence, much less actually be things that we can do together. But there are a growing number of bodybuilders who are jumping in on the idea of going on the vegan diet and using this as a way to help them to tone up and get the healthy nutrients that they need.

Yes, there is the traditional method of helping to bulk up and get stronger, and that involves eating a really high diet in animal fats and animal products. This is one way to do things, but it makes it more likely that the individual will deal with things like high blood pressure and high levels of cholesterol due to some of the unhealthy fats and other ingredients that are fond of some of those animal products.

With the vegan diet, we are able to cut out all of that bad stuff and still give the bodybuilder all of the nutrients and more that they need to do a great job with all of this. We are able to create some of the best results possible, even though we are switching over to a diet plan that is based on plants rather than one that is based on meats and animal products instead. Let's dive in a bit here and learn more about how we can make this work for some of our needs as well.

Contrary to some of the beliefs that are out there, it is possible for bodybuilders to go meat-free and still achieve all of their fitness goals. There is actually a lot of science out there that shows us how we are able to follow this kind of diet and actually achieve some of our goals much faster than before. Although a lot of people in the mainstream fitness community believe that bodybuilders have to consume a huge amount of animal proteins in order to bulk up and see any results, there are a lot of vegan bodybuilders out there. And many of them have been able to build up their own sexy and strong physiques while focusing on foods that are only based on plants.

For someone who is brand new to the whole idea of the vegan diet, it is easy to think that all that you need to do here is to cut out the cheese and the eggs in favor of some of the cherished snack foods instead. However, this style of dieting is going to add more flab to the body compared to the muscle tone that you are looking for. To help you to see some more bulk when it comes to veganism, you must make sure that you are going on a whole and healthy diet that will provide the body with all of the nutrients and more that it needs to survive.

Crafting a diet for bodybuilding that is vegan is so important. It is a bit of a challenge, though, and you need to have a lot of attention to detail, motivation, and knowledge about the diet plan to start with. Some of the basics and the guidelines that we need to follow in order to stick with the right nutrition for vegan bodybuilding will include:

1. Get the right calories

When you are going on this kind of diet, and you plan to be a bodybuilder, then you have to take in the right number of calories. The average vegan diet is going to be lower in calories than some of the conventional diets, so you need to really monitor your levels. If you do not take in enough calories, it is possible that your body is going to enter into a more catabolic state. The larger this deficit, the larger the problem is going to be. To get to your peak performance, you should go for 15 to 20 calories for each pound of bodyweight and then make some adjustments based on the noticeable losses and gains that you see in the gym.

2. Get the protein

While most of us need less protein than we think, it is still important for us to keep our protein levels at a good place, especially if we are doing bodybuilding. As long as you are keeping track of your protein levels and knowing which foods will have the best protein while still being a part of the vegan diet, you will be just fine.

3. Try some flax seed powder

In addition to the protein, another thing that you need to get in abundant amounts in your diet is lots of omega-3 fatty acids. And since you are not able to have fish on this kind of diet plan, going with the flax seed powder is going to be a good option. This is a good fiber profile and it is going to be a bit easier on the digestive system compared to flaxseed oil. It is going to give you the results that you want if you take it right when you wake up, right after you do some of the training, and right before you go to bed.

4. Take some Vegan BCAA

This is going to be a good option because it will protect your muscles from some of the catabolic effects that happen with a low-calorie diet and can be what you need to gain some more mass. In fact, according to one study in 2010 and published in Med Science Sports Exercise, the BCAA will help reduce the amount of soreness that you feel in the muscles when you are done training. For bodybuilding kinds of benefits, you should take some with your breakfast, some before and after training, and some before you go to bed.

5. Swap in some quinoa instead of rice.

You will find that rice will be one of the staples of this kind of diet plan, which means that it will be a really effective method to boost your nutritional intake and protein, and when you swap it out for some quinoa, these get even better. Quinoa will offer a higher quality of protein, and it is more of a complete source than brown rice. It also has a lot more of the nutrients that you need to fuel yourself after a workout. It even tastes and feels similar to what we are used to with brown rice, so it will not feel weird at all.

6. Choose some of the healthier drinks

Just because you are on the vegan diet doesn't mean that you have to spend your time filling the body with lots of sugary drinks with lots of calories and sugars and no Nutritional values per serving. You should keep things simple with a combination of protein shakes, water, tea, and coffee, and nothing else. Make sure that during this diet plan, you are staying as hydrated as possible to keep things running smoothly.

7. Look at some of the supplements for bodybuilding that are vegan

No conversations about this kind of diet and the exercise that you plan to do will be complete without us spending some time talking about the supplements. You will find that these nutritional supplements are going to be a requirement for those who want to body build in a competitive manner, and it is likely that this is a trend that is going to stick around for some time. There are a number of great supplements that can help out with this, and many of them are going to be considered vegan, so you know you are getting the best nutrition.

8. Address any of the deficiencies that will show up before they become damaging.

When you are going on this kind of diet plan, you need to make sure that you are getting all of the nutrients that you need to stay healthy. It is always a good idea to vary all of the foods and meals that you have in any diet plan because this will ensure that you are not going to suffer from a deficiency in any of them. This is especially true when you are taking the vegan diet like a bodybuilder. It also helps to make the diet more enjoyable overall. Some of the most common vegan deficiencies that you need to worry about will include the following:

1. Zinc
2. Calcium
3. Vitamin D
4. Vitamin B12
5. Omega-3 fatty acids
6. Iodine
7. Iron
8. Calories
9. Protein

If there is any time that you feel your body is starting to get low on one or more of these, then it is time to make some adjustments to your eating plan to make sure that you are able to get back on track. Going with a supplement can be a good option here as well.

As you can see, even bodybuilders are able to go through and follow the vegan diet for some of their needs as well. They may need to go through and create a few different options to ensure that they are getting the best results possible, but it is going to make it a whole lot easier to get some of the performance results that you want because you are actually feeding your body the healthy and wholesome foods and nutrients that it is looking for. The vegan diet is not necessarily the diet plan that most people think about when it comes to bodybuilding, but it is one of the best to choose to stick with.

PART II
RECIPES AND MEAL PLANS TO FUEL YOUR WORKOUTS

Chapter 5: The Meal Plan

It is at this point in the process where we need to take some time to talk about the meal plan. We have already taken a look at some of the basics of this kind of diet plan and what it is able to do for us. Even athletes are able to get a lot of benefits when they choose to work with the vegan diet, and we explored that a bit as well. As an athlete, though, you do need to take a few precautions along the way to ensure that you are picking out the right meals and the right amount of variety to ensure you get the nutrients your body needs.

This is probably one of the hardest parts of the whole diet. This is even truer when you are a beginner or when you are trying to get it to work around some of the more complicated nutrient requirements that athletes will sometimes have. This is why we will take some time in this chapter looking at the simple meal plan that you are able to follow to really do well on the vegan diet while being an athlete.

This meal plan is simple and easy to follow, and you will be able to make it work for your needs in no time. Let's take a look at the simple meal plan that athletes are able to follow when they are ready to be on the vegan meal plan.

Day 1:

Breakfast: Mexican Tofu Skillet
Lunch: Stuffed Hummus Pita Sandwich
Dinner: California Veggie Burger

Day 2:

Breakfast: Rolled oats with chia seeds and berries
Lunch: Curried Tofu Salad
Dinner: BBQ Tempeh

Day 3:

Breakfast: Vegan English Muffin
Lunch: Quinoa with spaghetti sauce and black beans
Dinner: Veggie burger

Day 4:

Breakfast: sweet potato toast with avocado
Lunch: Spinach and pepper salad
Dinner: Sweet Potato, Black Bean, and Quinoa Chili

Day 5:

Breakfast: Ezekiel toast with almond butter and apple
Lunch: Leafy green salad
Dinner: Grain Bowl

Blueberry Muffins

- ➤ Prep time 30 minutes
- ➤ Serves 8

Ingredients:
- ✓ Blueberries (1 c.)
- ✓ Baking soda (.5 tsp.)
- ✓ Flour (2 c.)
- ✓ Vanilla (1 tsp.)
- ✓ Maple syrup (.5 c)
- ✓ Applesauce (.5 c.)
- ✓ Milk that is plant-based (.5 c.)

Directions:
1. Turn on your oven and heat it up to 375 degrees. While the oven is heating up, bring out a big bowl and mix together the vanilla, maple syrup, applesauce, and milk.
2. When this is done, you can add in the flour and the baking soda, stirring until the batter is nice and smooth.
3. When you get the batter to be smooth, you can slowly add in the blueberries to make sure they get distributed through the batter.
4. Then take out a muffin tin and start adding the butter, filling up eight of the muffin cups until they are ¾ of the way full. Add to the oven.
5. After about 25 minutes, the muffins should be all done. You can take them out of the oven at that time and give them a few minutes to cool down before serving.

Nutritional values per serving:
Calories 200 - Carbs 45g - Fat 1g - Protein 4g

Banana Bread

> ➢ Cook time 60 minutes   ➢ Serves 8

Ingredients:
- ✓ Walnut pieces, optional (.25 c.)
- ✓ Baking soda (.5 tsp.)
- ✓ Cinnamon that is ground (.5 tsp.)
- ✓ Flour (1.5 c.)
- ✓ Vanilla (1 tsp.)
- ✓ Apple cider vinegar (1 Tbsp.)
- ✓ Maple syrup (.25 c.)
- ✓ Bananas that are ripe (4)

Directions:
1. To start this recipe, turn on the oven and let it heat up to 350 degrees.
2. While the oven is getting nice and warm, bring out a bowl and use a mixing spoon to mash up your bananas until they are pureed well. Stir in the vanilla, apple cider vinegar, and maple syrup at this time.
3. When this is done, you can stir in your baking soda, cinnamon, and flour. Fold in the pieces of walnuts if you are using them.
4. When all of this is combined into a nice batter, you can pour it into your prepared loaf pan and add it to the oven.
5. This needs to cook for a bit of time. After about 60 minutes or so, the bread should be done.
6. Take it out of the oven at this time and give it around half an hour to cool down before you serve.

Nutritional values per serving
Calories 178 - Carbs 40g - Fat 1g - Protein 4g

Pancakes

- ➢ Total time 30 min.
- ➢ Serves 4

Ingredients:
- ✓ Vanilla (1 tsp.)
- ✓ Maple syrup (.25 c)
- ✓ Applesauce (.5 c.)
- ✓ Milk that is plant-based (1 c.)
- ✓ Cinnamon that is ground (.5 tsp.)
- ✓ Baking powder (1 tsp.)
- ✓ Flour (1 c.)

Directions:
1. For this recipe, bring out a bowl and combine together the cinnamon, baking powder, and flour.
2. When those are well combined, you can stir in the vanilla, maple syrup, applesauce, and milk. You will want to stir these in until there isn't any more dry flour in there and the batter is nice and smooth.
3. When you are ready, heat up a skillet until it is nice and warm. To make each pancake, there should be eight total. You can add .25 cups of the batter onto the skillet.
4. Let it cook for a few minutes. When some bubbles start to form on the top, it is time to flip this around and cook for a bit longer.
5. Repeat the steps until you have been able to use up all of the batters and then serve.

Nutritional values per serving
Calories 219 - Carbs 44g - Fat 2g - Protein 5g

Pecan and Maple Granola

> ➢ Total time 25 minutes   ➢ Serves 4

Ingredients:
- ✓ Ground cinnamon (.5 tsp.)
- ✓ Maple syrup (.25 c)
- ✓ Vanilla (1 tsp.)
- ✓ Pecan pieces (.25 c.)
- ✓ Rolled oats (1.5 c.)

Directions:
1. Turn on the oven to start this and give it time to heat up to 300 degrees. While the oven is heating up, take out a baking sheet and line it with some parchment paper.
2. Then, take out a big bowl and combine together the cinnamon, vanilla, maple syrup, pecan pieces, and the oats. Stir these until the pecan pieces and the oats are coated all the way through.
3. When those are combined, you can spread this mixture out onto the baking sheet that you prepared ad then make it into an even layer. Add to the oven to bake.
4. After about 20 minutes, with a check on them at ten minutes, the granola should be all done. Take these out of the oven and let them set on the counter to cool down for a bit before serving.

Nutritional values per serving:
Calories 220 - Carbs 35g - Fat 7g - Protein 5g

Overnight Oatmeal

> ➢ Serves 2

Ingredients:
- ✓ Chia seeds (1 Tbsp.)
- ✓ Maple syrup (1 Tbsp.)
- ✓ Sliced banana (1)
- ✓ Pineapple chunks (.5 c.)
- ✓ Diced mango (.5 c.)
- ✓ Plant-based milk (2 c.)
- ✓ Rolled oats (2 c.)

Directions:
1. Bring out a big bowl and mix together the chia seeds, maple syrup, banana, pineapple, mango, milk, and oats.
2. When this is done, cover up the bowl and add it to the fridge. This needs to set for at least four hours, though leaving it to sit overnight is usually going to be the best.
3. The next morning you can take this out and serve.

Nutritional values per serving:
Calories 510
Carbs 93g
Fat 12g
Protein 14g

Pumpkin Pie Oatmeal

- ➢ Total time 35 minutes
- ➢ Serves 4

Ingredients:
- ✓ Ground nutmeg (.25 tsp.)
- ✓ Ground cloves (.25 tsp.)
- ✓ Ground cinnamon (1 tsp.)
- ✓ Maple syrup (2 Tbsp.)
- ✓ Unsweetened pumpkin puree (1 c.)
- ✓ Oats (1 c.)
- ✓ Milk that is plant-based (3 c.)

Directions:
1. Brin gout a pan and heat it up on medium heat. Add the milk inside and then let this come to a boil.
2. When the milk is to a rolling boil, you can reduce the heat down to a low ad then stir in the nutmeg, cloves, cinnamon, maple syrup, oats, and pumpkin puree.
3. When all of those are in the pot, cover it up and let these cook for a bit. You will want to stop and stir it every few minutes to help keep it mixed and to make sure that none of the oatmeal is able to stick to the bottom.
4. After about half an hour, this mixture should be done. Pour it into a few bowls before serving.

Nutritional values per serving:
Calories 218
Carbs 38g
Fat 5g
Protein 7g

Peanut Butter and Chocolate Quinoa

- ➢ Total time 25 minutes
- ➢ Serves 2

Ingredients:
- ✓ Peanut powder (1 Tbsp.)
- ✓ Cocoa powder (1 Tbsp.)
- ✓ Maple syrup (1 Tbsp.)
- ✓ Cooked quinoa (2 c.)
- ✓ Milk that is based on plants (1 c.)

Directions:
1. Take the time to cook up the quinoa. You can follow the instructions that are on the back of the box that came with it to make this easier.
2. When that is done, bring out another pan and heat it up. Add the milk inside and bring this to a boil as well.
3. When the milk is at a rolling boil, then it is time to reduce the heat a bit to a low setting before adding in the peanut powder, cocoa powder, maple syrup, and the quinoa.
4. Cook these for a bit without the lid on top. After five minutes, with a constant stream of stirring the whole time, you can serve this mixture nice and warm.

Nutritional values per serving:
Calories 339
Carbs 52g
Fat 8g
Protein 14g

Early Morning Scramble

> ➢ Total time 30 minutes
> ➢ Serves 2

Ingredients:
- ✓ Spinach, fresh (1 c.0 pepper
- ✓ Onion powder (.5 tsp.)
- ✓ Garlic powder (.5 tsp.)
- ✓ Vegetable broth or water (1 Tbsp.)
- ✓ Nutritional yeast (2 Tbsp.)
- ✓ Diced bell pepper (.5)
- ✓ Sliced mushrooms (4 oz)
- ✓ Tofu (14 oz.)

Directions:
1. Start out this recipe by taking out a skillet and heat it on the stove.
2. You can drain out your tofu package and then add it into the skillet, mashing it down with a fork or your mashing spoon.
3. When this is done, we can stir in the pepper, onion powder, garlic powder, broth, nutritional yeast, bell pepper, and mushrooms.
4. When all of those are in the skillet, you can cover up the pan and cook for a bit, making sure to stir a few times as well.
5. After ten minutes, you can uncover the pot and then stir in the spinach—Cook for a few more minutes before serving this warm.

Nutritional values per serving:
Calories 230
Carbs 16g
Fat 10g
Protein 27g

Loaded Breakfast Burrito

- ➢ Total time 30 min.
- ➢ Serves 2

Ingredients:
- ✓ 6 corn tortillas
- ✓ Salsa(.25 c.)
- ✓ Onion powder (.5 tsp.)
- ✓ Garlic powder (.5 tsp.)
- ✓ Nutritional yeast (1 Tbsp.)
- ✓ Vegetable broth or water (2 Tbsp.)
- ✓ Diced and seeded jalapeno (1)
- ✓ Sliced mushrooms (4 oz.)
- ✓ Cooked black beans (1 c.)
- ✓ Diced potatoes (2)
- ✓ Firm tofu (.5 block)

Directions:
1. The first step is to heat up a skillet on the stove and let it get nice and warm.
2. When that is done you can drain out the tofu that you are using and then place it into that pan, mashing it down with a mixing spoon or your form.
3. After this, take the onion powder, garlic powder, nutritional yeast, broth, jalapeno, mushrooms, black beans, and potatoes and add them into that warm skillet.
4. When the ingredients are all inside, you can reduce the heat to a low setting and then covers up the skillet. Cook until the potatoes are nice and soft and can be pierced using a fork.
5. After ten minutes, this part should be done. You can take the cover off the skillet and add in the salsa to heat up. After ten minutes, those should be done as well.
6. Now it is time to warm up the tortillas. Add to the microwave and heat up for 15 to 30 seconds each until they are soft or warm.
7. Take the skillet from the heat and add about 1/6 of the filling into the middle of your tortilla. Roll these up and serve them nice and warm.

Nutritional values per serving:
Calories 535 - Carbs 95g - Fat 8g - Protein 29g

Sweet Potato Skillet

> Total time 30 minutes

> Serves 4

Ingredients:

- ✓ Pepper
- ✓ Chili powder (.5 tsp.)
- ✓ Ground cumin (.5 tp.)
- ✓ Vegetable broth (1 c.)
- ✓ Diced sweet onion (1)
- ✓ Diced bell pepper (1)
- ✓ Sliced mushrooms (8 oz.)
- ✓ Diced sweet potatoes (4)

Directions:

1. Bring out a skillet and give it some time to heat up on the stove.
2. Once you have the time to get the skillet nice and hot, add in the pepper, chili powder, cumin, garlic powder, broth, onion, bell pepper, mushrooms, and sweet potatoes in as well.
3. Cover up the skillet and then let this cook for a bit until the sweet potatoes are all done and we can pierce them easily with a fork.
4. This will all take about ten minutes. When that time is up, take the cover off the skillet and give it a stir. Add in a bit of the broth if needed to get the ingredients to not be stuck on the bottom.
5. Cook without the cover for another five minutes before serving this dish nice and warm.

Nutritional values per serving:

Calories 158

Carbs 34g

Fat 1g

Protein 6g

Vegan Omelet

- ➢ Prep time 30 minutes
- ➢ Serves 2

Ingredients:
- ✓ Nutritional yeast (4 Tbsp.)
- ✓ Minced garlic cloves (4)
- ✓ Hummus (4 Tbsp.)
- ✓ Silken tofu (10 oz.)
- ✓ Arrowroot powder (2 tsp.)
- ✓ Paprika (.5 tsp.)
- ✓ Pepper and Salt

For the filling:
- ✓ Vegetables of choice (2 c.)
- ✓ *For the toppings*
- ✓ Vegan parmesan cheese
- ✓ Salsa
- ✓ Herbs

Directions:
1. Start this recipe by turning on the oven and heating it up to 375 degrees. While this is heating up, you can prepare the vegetables to mince the garlic and dry off the tofu before putting it all to the side.
2. Then take out a skillet and heat it up. Add in the garlic and the oil and let it cook for just a few minutes.
3. Add this to the blender along with the rest of the ingredients for the omelet. If you need to thin it out a bit you can add a bit of water at a time.
4. Add some more oil to your skillet, and then put the vegetables in as well. These need to go for about 5 minutes.
5. When that time is done, take the skillet off the heat and see that it has enough oil so the omelet is not going to stick. Spoon the batter of the omelet into it along with a bit of the cooked vegetables.
6. Put this back on the stove and cook until you see the edges are starting to dry. After five minutes, add to the oven to finish cooking.
7. After 10 minutes or so, the omelet should be golden brown and done. You can, during the final few minutes, you can add the vegetables back to the top of the omelet and cook for a bit longer.
8. Remove this out of the oven when the time is done and then fold it over with a spatula before serving.

Nutritional values per serving:
Calories 232 - Carbs 22g - Fat 7.8g - Protein 22g

BBQ Sauce

- ➢ Prep time 5 minutes
- ➢ Serves 12

Ingredients:

- ✓ Tomato sauce, sweet (18 oz.)
- ✓ Maple syrup (2 Tbsp.)
- ✓ Apple cider vinegar (1 Tbsp.)
- ✓ Soy sauce, low in sodium (1.5 Tbsp.)
- ✓ Chili flakes (1 tsp.)
- ✓ Sweet paprika (.5 Tbsp.)
- ✓ Smoked paprika (.5 Tbsp)
- ✓ Dried oregano (.5 tsp)
- ✓ Liquid smoke (.5 tsp.)

Directions:

1. To start this recipe, bring out a bowl and then make sure that all of the ingredients are thrown into it together.
2. You should do some whisking on this until there are no longer any lumps found inside.
3. When this is done, add to a container for about 60 minutes or so before using, or store in the fridge to use later.

Nutritional values per serving:

Calories 12
Carbs 2.3g
Fat 0.1g
Protein 0.4g

Your Own Marinara Sauce

- ➢ Prep time 40 minutes
- ➢ Serves 13

Ingredients:
- ✓ Diced tomatoes (4 big cans)
- ✓ Chopped basil (1 c.)
- ✓ Olive oil (4 Tbsp.)
- ✓ Nutritional yeast (4 Tbsp.)
- ✓ Garlic cloves (6)
- ✓ Oregano, dried (2 tsp.)
- ✓ Maple syrup (1.5 Tbsp.)
- ✓ Cayenne pepper (.5 tsp.)
- ✓ Salt if you would like

Directions:
1. To start this recipe, take out a big pot and heat it up. When the pot is warm, add in the oil and warm it up with the minced garlic cloves and cook around.
2. After a minute of cooking the garlic, you can continue on by adding in the tomatoes, oregano, cayenne pepper, and then the maple syrup. Add in the amount of salt that you want.
3. It is time to bring all of this to a simmer. Reduce the heat to a lower setting and then cover up the pot. Simmer these ingredients to cook well.
4. After 25 minutes, this should be nice and warm and it is time to add in the basil and then the nutritional yeast. Stir it around and add in some more of the salt and the water if you would like.
5. Store away to use on a dish in the future or add it to your favorite dish.

Nutritional values per serving:
Calories 65
Carbs 5g
Fat 4g
Protein 1.5g

Taco Salsa

- ➢ Prep time 10 minutes
- ➢ Serves 6

Ingredients:
- ✓ Pepper and salt to your taste
- ✓ Lime (1)
- ✓ Chopped cilantro (2 Tbsp.)
- ✓ Red onion (.5)
- ✓ Jalapeno (1)
- ✓ Firm tomatoes (4)

Directions:
1. Start off by skinning and then seeding your tomatoes. We can then take the jalapeno and remove the stem and the seeds.
2. Then it is time to cut both of these, the jalapeno and the tomatoes, and dice into some fine pieces before adding to a bowl.
3. Now it is time to chop up both your red onion and your cilantro before adding into a bowl. And then juice your lime and add all of that juice into your bowl as well.
4. You can now mix the ingredients and then season with some pepper and salt. Let it marinate together for about 60 minutes before serving.

Nutritional values per serving:
Calories 30
Carbs 6.1g
Fat 0.3g
Protein 0.8g

Apple Sauce

- ➢ Prep time 40 minutes
- ➢ Serves 4

Ingredients:
- ✓ Lemon juice (1 Tbsp.)
- ✓ Cinnamon (.5 tsp.)
- ✓ Salt (1 pinch)
- ✓ Water (.5 c.)
- ✓ Peeled and quartered delicious red apples (4)
- ✓ Peeled and quartered Jazz apples (4)

Directions:
1. Take the apples and add them to some colder water. This needs to happen for at least 5 minutes or so.
2. When that time is done, we can take the apples out of our water and then slice them all up into quarters.
3. Add these slices into a pan and then cook them with a bit of water and some salt.
4. Stir this often so that it does not burn, and bring it to a simmer right after you notice it is cooking.
5. When ten minutes of cooking is done, you can mash up the apples while they are still in simmering mode because this will create the sauce.
6. Continue to strand do some mashing in this manner until you have applesauce that is chunky. This will take us around 20 minutes to accomplish.
7. Add in the lemon juice and cinnamon at this point and allow it some time to cool down.
8. If you would like to have it be a bit smoother, you can add it to the blender to make it that way before serving.

Nutritional values per serving:
Calories 202
Carbs 50.5g
Fat 0g
Protein 0g

Vegan Mayo

- ➢ Prep time 10 minutes
- ➢ Serves 6

Ingredients:
- ✓ Garlic cloves (1)
- ✓ MCT oil (1 c.)
- ✓ Lemon juice (1 tsp.)
- ✓ Almond milk (.5 c.)
- ✓ Agave nectar (1 tsp.)
- ✓ Rice vinegar (1 tsp.)
- ✓ Ground mustard (.5 tsp.)
- ✓ Onion powder (1 tsp.)
- ✓ Chili powder (1 tsp.)
- ✓ Paprika powder (1 tsp.)
- ✓ Garlic clove (1)

Directions:
1. Take out a blender and add in all of the almond milk, mustard, rice vinegar, agave nectar, onion powder, chili powder, paprika, and garlic. Blend to make smooth.
2. Slowly add in the MCT oil to this and blend to make the almond milk and the oil come together well.
3. When you notice that this mixture is starting to get a bit thicker, you can add in some of the lemon juice. Then store this into a glass jar that is sealable before serving.

Nutritional values:
Calories 344
Carbs 1.3g
Fat 38g
Protein 0g

Easy Enchilada Sauce

- ➤ Prep time 10 minutes
- ➤ Serves 13

Ingredients:
- ✓ MCT oil (1.5 Tbsp.)
- ✓ Chili powder (.5 Tbsp.)
- ✓ Whole wheat flour (.5 Tbsp.)
- ✓ Ground cumin (.5 tsp)
- ✓ Dried or fresh oregano (.25 tsp.)
- ✓ Salt (.25 tsp.)
- ✓ Minced garlic clove (1)
- ✓ Tomato paste of choice (1 Tbsp.)
- ✓ Vegetable broth (1 c.)
- ✓ Apple cider vinegar (.5 tsp.)
- ✓ Pepper (.5 tsp.)

Directions:
1. Take out a pan and let it heat up on the stove. Wen that is warmed up, you can throw in the minced garlic and the MCT oil and cook these around for 60 seconds or so.
2. Then it is time to bring out a bowl and mix together the flour along with all of the dry spices. Pour the dry mixture into the saucepan.
3. When that is done, stir in the tomato paste and then slowly pour in your vegetable broth at the same time, stirring to make sure that it is all going to come in as we want.
4. When this is thoroughly mixed together well, we can increase the heat a bit and let this simmer, so the sauce has the time to thicken.
5. After three minutes of cooking, we can take the pan from the heat we are using and add in the pepper and the vinegar before storing or serving.

Nutritional values per serving
Calories 18 - Carbs 0.6g - Fat 1.6g - Protein 0.1g

BBQ Sliders

- ➢ Total time 30 minutes
- ➢ Serves 6

Ingredients:
- ✓ Tomatoes, pickles, onions for topping
- ✓ Asian style slaw for topping
- ✓ Slider buns (6)
- ✓ Onion powder (1 tsp.)
- ✓ Garlic powder (1 tsp.)
- ✓ BBQ sauce (.5 c.)
- ✓ Green jackfruit (2 cans)

Directions:
1. Bring out a big bowl and use a fork or your own potato masher to help get the jackfruit mashed to a shredded type of consistency.
2. Heat up a stockpot and add in the onion powder, garlic powder, BBQ sauce, and shredded jackfruit.
3. Stir this around and cover the pot. After 10 minutes, then you can take the lid off.
4. If you notice that the jackfruit is starting to stick, then you can add in a bit of water or vegetable broth to help with this.
5. When the lid is off, you can cook for a few more minutes to heat all the way up.
6. Serve this on some of the slider buns and add on your favorite toppings before serving.

Nutritional values per serving
Calories 188
Carbs 36g
Fat 2g
Protein 7g

Hawaiian Burgers

- ➢ Total time 30 min.
- ➢ Serves 8

Ingredients:
- ✓ Toppings of your choice
- ✓ Buns (8)
- ✓ Pineapple sliced into rings (1)
- ✓ Onion powder (1 tsp.)
- ✓ Garlic powder (1 tsp.)
- ✓ Pineapple juice (.25 c.)
- ✓ BBQ sauce (.25 c.)
- ✓ Oats that are quick-cooking (1 .c)
- ✓ Cooked brown rice (2 c.)
- ✓ Cooked black beans (3 c.)

Directions:
1. Turn on the grill at the beginning of this and get it up to medium-high heat.
2. In the meantime, take out a bowl and use a fork to help mash the black beans in. then add in the onion powder, garlic powder, pineapple juice, BBQ sauce, oats, and rice into it.
3. Combine this mixture until it is able to hold its own shape and can be formed into patties.
4. Scoop out about half a cup of this and form into a patty. Repeat to use up the whole mixture and then add these onto the grill.
5. Cook for about 5 minutes on the one side and then flip them over to cook on that side.
6. Add the pineapple rings on the grill at this time and only cook for a few minutes on each side.
7. When this is done, take the pineapple rings and burgers off the grill. Add one pineapple ring and one patty onto each bun.
8. Top with some of the BBQ sauce and some of the favorite toppings you chose before serving.

Nutritional values per serving
Calories 371 - Carbs 71g - Fat 3g - Protein 15g

Falafel Burgers

> Total time 30 min.   > Serves 8

Ingredients:
- ✓ Favorite toppings
- ✓ Whole-wheat buns or pita pockets
- ✓ Ground pepper (.25 tsp.)
- ✓ Ground coriander (1 tsp.)
- ✓ Ground cumin (1.5 tsp.)
- ✓ Onion powder (2 tsp.)
- ✓ Garlic powder (2 tsp.)
- ✓ Lemon juice (1 Tbsp.)
- ✓ Chopped parsley that is fresh (.25 c.)
- ✓ Vegetable broth (.25 c.)
- ✓ Brown rice that is cooked (2 c.)
- ✓ Cooked chickpeas (3 c.)

Directions:
1. Turn on the oven and let it heat up to 425 degrees. While the oven is heating up you can take out a baking sheet and line with some parchment paper.
2. Now bring out your food processor and combine the pepper, coriander, onion powder, cumin, garlic powder, lemon juice, parsley, broth, rice, and chickpeas.
3. Process these ingredients together for about half a minute. You don't want it to turn into hummus but have it enough so that it forms into patties.
4. When this is done take about half a cup of the mixture and form it into patties. Add onto your prepared baking sheet and then repeat that with the rest of the mixture.
5. Add this to the oven and let it bake. After 15 minutes, take these out of the oven and then flip them around before cooking for another 15 minutes.
6. When this is done, take the patties out of the oven to cool down. Fill up the buns or the pitas with some of your favorite toppings and then add in the burgers to serve.

Nutritional values per serving
Calories 230 - Carbs 44g - Total 3g - Protein 10g

Vegan Pizza Bread

> ➢ Total time 45 minutes
> ➢ Serves 4

Ingredients:
- ✓ Garlic powder (.5 tsp.)
- ✓ Onion powder (.5 tsp.)
- ✓ Nutritional yeast (1 tsp.)
- ✓ Marinara (1 c.)
- ✓ An unsliced loaf of bread (1)

Directions:
1. Turn on the oven and heat it up to 375 degrees.
2. While that is warming up, halve the loaf of bread going lengthwise. Ten spread out the marinara on top f each part before sprinkling on the garlic powder, onion powder, and nutritional yeast.
3. Add the bread onto your prepared baking sheet and then add it into the oven to bake.
4. After 20 minutes, the bread is going to be light and golden brown and you can let it have some time to cool down before serving.

Nutritional values per serving
Calories 230
Carbs 38g
Fat 3g
Protein 13g

Baked Mac and Peas

- ➢ Total time 60 minutes
- ➢ Serves 8

Ingredients:
- ✓ Green peas (2 c.)
- ✓ Anytime vegan cheese sauce (1 recipe)
- ✓ Macaroni pasta (16 oz.)

Directions:
1. Turn on the oven and give it time to heat up to 400 degrees.
2. While the oven is getting nice and warm, bring out a big stockpot with some water and use it to cook the pasta until it is al dente. Drain out the pasta and the water when it is done.
3. Then bring out a big baking dish and add the cooked pasta along with the peas and the sauce, making sure to mix well. Add into the oven to bake.
4. After 30 minutes the dish should be a nice golden brown and this is the sign that it is done and ready to take out.
5. Bring it out of the oven and let it cool down before you serve.

Nutritional values per serving
Calories 209
Carbs 42g
Fat 3g
Protein 12g

Sweet Potato Casserole

> ➢ Total time 45 minutes
> ➢ Serves 6

Ingredients:
- ✓ Dried rosemary (1 tsp.)
- ✓ Dried thyme (1 tsp.)
- ✓ Dried sage (1 Tbsp.)
- ✓ Vegetable broth (.5 c.)
- ✓ Cooked sweet potatoes (8)

Directions:
1. Turn on the oven and let it heat up to 375 degrees.
2. While the oven is getting nice and warm, remove and throw out the skins from your sweet potatoes and then add the potatoes into your baking dish.
3. Mash these up with a potato masher or a fork and then stir in the rosemary, sage, thyme, and broth.
4. Add this into the oven and give it some time to bake. After 30 minutes, the sweet potatoes should be done and you can serve warm.

Nutritional values per serving:
Calories 154
Carbs 35g
Fat 0g
Protein 3g

Sunday Roast

- ➢ Total Time 4 to 6 hours
- ➢ Serves 8

Ingredients:
- ✓ Pepper (1 tsp.)
- ✓ Garlic powder (1 tsp.)
- ✓ Onion powder (1 tsp.)
- ✓ Vegetable broth (4 c.)
- ✓ Sliced mushrooms (8 oz.)
- ✓ Green beans (12 oz.)
- ✓ Sweet onion cubed (3)
- ✓ Sliced carrots (6)
- ✓ Cubed white potatoes (6)

Directions:
1. When you are ready, take out your slow cooker and get it all set up and ready to go.
2. Then add the pepper, garlic powder, onion powder, broth, mushrooms, green beans, onions, carrots, and potatoes inside. Stir these together well to get the spices to mix in.
3. Add the lid on top and then cook this for four hours on a high setting or six hours on a low setting.
4. Make sure to stir the ingredients together well before serving.

Nutritional values per serving
Calories 190
Carbs 39g
Fat 1g
Protein 8g

Vegetable Stir-Fry

> ➢ Total time 30 minutes
> ➢ Serves 4

Ingredients:
- ✓ Cooked brown rice (4)
- ✓ Onion powder (1 tsp.)
- ✓ Garlic powder (1 tsp.)
- ✓ Water or vegetable broth (.25 c.)
- ✓ Green beans (2 c.)
- ✓ Green peas (2 c.)

Directions:
1. To start, bring out a pan and heat it up on the stove. When it is warm, you can add in the onion powder, garlic powder, broth, green beans, and peas. Stir it all around.
2. Cover the pan and then let these cook for a bit. Make sure to stir on a regular basis as well.
3. After 8 minutes you can uncover the pan and add in the brown rice that is already cooked. Let these cook for a bit longer.
4. After 5 minutes, with constant stirring in the meantime, this is going to be ready to serve.

Nutritional values per serving
Calories 233; Carbs 48g; Fat 2g; Protein 8g

Vegetable Spring Rolls with Sauce

- ➤ Total time 30 min.
- ➤ Serves 2

Ingredients:

- ✓ *Dipping sauce*
- ✓ red pepper flakes (.5 tsp.)
- ✓ garlic powder (.5 tsp.)
- ✓ onion powder (.5 tsp.)
- ✓ rice vinegar (1 Tbsp.)
- ✓ maple syrup (1 Tbsp.)
- ✓ peanut powder (2 Tbsp.)

For the spring rolls:

- ✓ Brown rice, cooked (1.5 c.)
- ✓ Lettuce leaves (6)
- ✓ Rice paper wraps (6)
- ✓ Fresh basil (1 bunch)
- ✓ Fresh mint (1 bunch)
- ✓ Fresh cilantro (1 bunch)
- ✓ Shredded carrots (1 c.)

Directions:

1. We can start with the dipping sauce. To do this, we can take out a pan and heat it up.
2. Add in the red pepper flakes, garlic powder onion powder, rice vinegar, maple syrup, and peanut powder.
3. Cook these in the pan for about 10 minutes, making sure to stir on occasion. After the ten minutes, take off the heat and set to the side to cool down a bit.
4. Bring out a shallow bowl or a pan and pour in a bit of water that is warm. Dip a rice paper wrap into the bowl for about ten seconds.
5. Add to a cutting board or another smooth surface. Then lay a lettuce leaf down flat on the rice paper and add .25 cup of the prepared brown rice to it.
6. Top with some of the shredded carrots and a few leaves of each the basil, mint, and cilantro.
7. Wrap the sides of the rice paper right in the center and then rolls up the wrap from the bottom to the top to make the roll tight. Repeat for the rest of your spring rolls.
8. Serve this with the sauce in a bowl on the side and enjoy it.

Nutritional values per serving

Calories 263 - Carbs 46g - Fat 3g - Protein 11g

Orange Tofu Bowl

> Total Time 40 min.

> Serves 4

Ingredients:

For the tofu:
- ✓ Cubed tofu (14 oz)
- ✓ Ground pepper (.5 tsp.)
- ✓ Onion powder (1 tsp.)
- ✓ Garlic powder (1 tsp.)
- ✓ Flour (.25 c.)

For the orange glaze:
- ✓ Onion powder (.5 tsp.)
- ✓ Garlic powder (.5 tsp.)
- ✓ Maple syrup (1 Tbsp.)
- ✓ Rice vinegar (1 Tbsp.)
- ✓ Cornstarch (1 Tbsp.)
- ✓ Orange juice (.5 c.)

For the bowl:
> Brown rice, cooked (6 c.)

Directions:

1. We are going to start by making the tofu part. Start by heating up the oven so that it can reach 400 degrees. While the oven is heating up, line a baking sheet with some parchment paper.
2. In the meantime, take out a bowl and whisk together the pepper, onion powder, garlic powder, and flour. Toss the tofu here and toss to cover completely.
3. Add this to the baking sheet and into the oven to bake for a bit. After 20 minutes turn it around and bake for another 20 minutes before bringing out.
4. Then it is time to make the orange glaze. While your tofu is in the oven, bring out a pan and combine the onion powder, garlic powder, maple syrup, rice vinegar, cornstarch and orange juice inside.
5. Bring this to a boil and then when it reaches that, reduce the heat and simmer for a bit.
6. After ten minutes, take the glaze off the heat and set it to the side.
7. Now it is time to make the bowl. Take the tofu out of the oven and mix it nicely and gently with the orange glaze.
8. When you are ready to serve, put 1.5 cups of the brown rice into a bowl and then top with about 1/4th of the orange glaze and tofu here. Serve warm.

Nutritional values per serving

Calories 380 - Carbs 65g - Fat 8g - Protein 15g

Mango Chickpea Curry

- ➢ Total time 30 minutes
- ➢ Serves 6

Ingredients:
- ✓ Ground cinnamon (.25 tsp.)
- ✓ Onion powder (1 tsp.)
- ✓ Garlic powder (1 tsp.)
- ✓ Ground coriander (1 tsp.)
- ✓ Curry powder (1 Tbsp.)
- ✓ Ground ginger (1 Tbsp.)
- ✓ Maple syrup (2 Tbsp.)
- ✓ Milk that is plant-based (2 c.)
- ✓ Mango chunks (2 c.)
- ✓ Cooked chickpeas (3 c.)

Directions:
1. Take out a big stockpot and heat it up on the oven.
2. In this post, you can add in the cinnamon, onion powder, garlic powder, coriander, ginger, curry powder, maple syrup, milk mango, and the chickpeas.
3. After stirring, you can cover up the pot and let it cook, making sure to stir a few times
4. After 10 minutes, you can take the lid off the pot and let it cook a few more minutes before serving warm.

Nutritional values per serving
Calories 219 - Carbs 38g - Fat 4g - Protein 8g

Italian Bean Balls

- ➢ Total time 30 min.
- ➢ Serves 6

Ingredients:
- ✓ Pepper (.25 tsp.)
- ✓ Onion powder (1 tsp.)
- ✓ Garlic powder (1 tsp.)
- ✓ Italian seasoning (1 Tbsp.)
- ✓ Marinara (.25 c.)
- ✓ Oats that are quick-cooking (1 c.)
- ✓ Brown rice that is cooked (1 c.)
- ✓ Red kidney beans that are cooked (1.5 c.)
- ✓ Cooked black beans (1.5 c.)

Directions:
1. Turn on the oven and let it heat up to 400 degrees. While the oven is heating up, you can line a baking sheet with a bit of parchment paper.
2. Takeout a big bowl and add the kidney beans and black beans together. Use a fork to help mash these together well.
3. Now add in the pepper, onion powder, garlic powder, Italian seasoning, marinara, oats, and rice and stir them together well to combine.
4. Scoop out about .25 c of the bean mixture and then work to make this into a ball. Add these balls onto your baking sheet.
5. Make sure to repeat these steps with the rest of the bean mixture, leaving enough space so they are not touching. Add the prepared baking sheet into the oven to bake.
6. After half an hour, these balls should be browned and heated all the way through. When this happens, take the balls out of the oven and let them cool before serving with a salad or some vegetables.

Nutritional values per serving
Calories 144 - Carbs 26g - Fat 2g - Protein 6g

Crispy Chicken Salad

> ➢ Prep time 20 minutes   ➢ Serves 2

Ingredients:
- ✓ Vegan mayo (2 Tbsp.)
- ✓ Vegan crispy chicken (300 g)
- ✓ Sliced tomato (.5)
- ✓ Sliced lettuce (.25)

Directions:
1. To start this recipe, turn on the oven and let it heat up to 350 degrees. When that is all warmed up, add the vegan chicken to the oven and let it cook for a bit.
2. After 15 minutes, the chicken should be done and you can set it to the side to cool down.
3. While the chicken is cooking or cooling down, you can take the tomato and lettuce and chop it up.
4. When it is all done you can add the vegetables to a bowl with the chicken and stir together with the mayo before serving.

Nutritional values per serving
Calories 305
Carbs 17g
Fat 15g
Protein 20g

Arugula and Lentil Salad

> ➢ Prep time 12 minutes

> ➢ Serves 2

Ingredients:

- ✓ Pepper
- ✓ Salt
- ✓ Balsamic vinegar (2 Tbsp.)
- ✓ Arugula (1 handful)
- ✓ Cooked brown lentils (1 c.)
- ✓ Whole wheat bread (3 slices)
- ✓ Sun-dried tomatoes in oil (5)
- ✓ Jalapeno (1)
- ✓ Olive oil (3 Tbsp.)
- ✓ Onion (1)
- ✓ Cashews (.75 c.)

Directions:

1. You can start this recipe by roasting the cashew nuts in a pan for about 3 minutes with the help of a bit of oil. When you are done with these, add them into a big salad bowl for now.
2. Then it is time to dice up the onion and fry for a few minutes, usually around three, with another bit of the oil.
3. As your onion is frying, it is time to chop up the tomatoes and chili and add them to a pan to fry for a bit longer. You can then take these when they are done and add them to the bowl with the cashews.
4. You can then take the bread and chop it into some croutons before frying up in the rest of the oil to make it nice and crunchy. When those are done, add them to the salad bowl as well.
5. Take the arugula and the lentils and add them to this bowl. You need to mix the ingredients well together and season with some salt, vinegar, and pepper. Serve right away.

Nutritional values per serving
Calories 663
Carbs 64g
Fat 41g
Protein 25g

Quinoa and Vegetables

> ➢ Prep time 25 minutes
> ➢ Serves 3

Ingredients:
- ✓ Basil or parsley
- ✓ Green onions (4)
- ✓ Corn (1.5 c.)
- ✓ Orange bell pepper (1)
- ✓ Roma tomatoes (3)
- ✓ Garbanzo beans (15 oz.)
- ✓ Uncooked white quinoa (1 c.)

For the dressing:
- ✓ Olive oil (1 Tbsp.)
- ✓ Basil (1.5 tsp.)
- ✓ Lemon juice (2 Tbsp.)

Directions:
1. To start this recipe, you can bring out the quinoa and then follow the directions on the package in order to cook it all up.
2. While your quinoa is cooking, you can whisk together the ingredients that you are using for the dressing and then set to the side.
3. Now we can chop up the tomatoes, pepper, and onions. You can also rinse out and drain the garbanzo beans.
4. Pop your quinoa when it is done into a big bowl and then top with the ingredients for the salad. Pour the dressing on top and stir around to combine well before serving.

Nutritional values:
Calories 488
Carbs 76g
Fat 12g
Protein 18g

Chickpea Sunflower Sandwich

 ➢ Prep time 20 minutes
 ➢ Serves 2

Ingredients:
For the sandwich:
 ✓ Lettuce, tomato, onion, and avocado for toppings
 ✓ Rustic bread (4 pieces)
 ✓ Pinch of salt and pepper
 ✓ Chopped dill (2 Tbsp.)
 ✓ Chopped red onion (.25 c.)
 ✓ Dijon mustard (.5 tsp.)
 ✓ Vegan mayo (3 Tbsp.)
 ✓ Sunflower seeds (.25 c.)
 ✓ Chickpeas (15 oz.)
Garlic herb sauce:
 ✓ Almond milk
 ✓ Minced garlic cloves (2)
 ✓ Dried dill (1 tsp.)
 ✓ Half of a lemon juiced
 ✓ Hummus (.25 c.)

Directions:
1. Mix together all of the ingredients that you will use for the garlic and herb sauce and then set it to the side.
2. You can then add your chickpeas to a bowl and mash it up with a fork for the right texture. Then add in the pepper, salt, dill, red onion, maple syrup, mayo mustard, and sunflower seeds to the mix. Adjust the seasonings to help the taste.
3. You can then take the time to toast the bread and the other toppings of the sandwich such as the lettuce, onion, and tomato.
4. Scoop a good amount of this filling and add to the bread. Add with some of the sauce and toppings that you want and then add on the other two slices of bread before serving.

Chickpea and Lentil Bowl

- ➢ Prep time 45 minutes
- ➢ Serves 4

Ingredients:
- ✓ Salt (1 tsp.)
- ✓ Curry powder (.5 tsp.)
- ✓ Garam Masala seasoning (2 tsp.)
- ✓ Drained chickpeas (15 oz.)
- ✓ Diced Roma tomatoes (2)
- ✓ Water (1 c.)
- ✓ Vegetable broth (2 c.)
- ✓ Vegan milk (1 c.)
- ✓ Dried red lentils (1.5 c.)
- ✓ Diced onion (.5 c.)
- ✓ Chopped carrots (2)

Directions:
1. Take the time to fill up a pan and add in some water. Let it get to boiling and then add in the carrots. After five minutes or so of cooking, drain out the water and set the carrots to the side.
2. While your carrots are boiling, you can heat up a bit of oil in a pan and then add in the onion. Cook for a bit so that the onion can become translucent.
3. In another pan, add in the chickpeas, carrots, milk, water, broth, lentils, and onions together. Season with the spices as well.
4. Bring this to a boil and when it reaches that point, you can reduce the heat a bit and let these ingredients simmer together.
5. After 20 minutes, you can take the whole skillet from the heat and serve it warm.

Nutritional values per serving:
Calories 470 - Carbs 79g - Fat 5g - Protein 32g

Vegan Chicken, Tomato and Lettuce Sandwich

> ➢ Prep time 20 minutes
> ➢ Serves 2

Ingredients:
- ✓ Vegan mayo to serve
- ✓ Tomato slices (4)
- ✓ Lettuce leaves (2)
- ✓ Chicken bites, crispy (8)
- ✓ Slices of bread (4)

Directions:
1. Start this recipe by turning on the oven and giving it time to heat up to 350 degrees. Add the vegan chicken to a baking pan and add to the oven to bake.
2. After 15 minutes, the chicken should be done. While those are cooking, you can take the time to slice the tomato and pull off the lettuce leaves that you need.
3. Add some butter and mayo to your slices of bread. Then add on the cooked nuggets to the sandwich and enjoy it when ready.

Nutritional values per serving
Calories 461
Carbs 20g
Fat24g
Protein 17g

Tempeh and Carrot Salad

- ➢ Prep time 20 minutes
- ➢ Serves 4

Ingredients:

- ✓ Liquid smoke (.25 tsp.)
- ✓ Sliced tempeh (8 oz.)
- ✓ Pepper
- ✓ Salt
- ✓ Cayenne (2 pinches)
- ✓ Parsley (.5 c.)
- ✓ Maple syrup (1 Tbsp.)
- ✓ Lemon juice (.25 c.)
- ✓ Tahini (2 Tbsp.)
- ✓ Pepper (.25 tsp.)
- ✓ Turmeric powder (.25 tsp.)
- ✓ Curry powder (1 Tbsp.)
- ✓ Diced onion (1)
- ✓ Shredded carrots (4 c.)
- ✓ Raw walnuts (1 Tbsp.)
- ✓ Soy sauce (2 tsp.)
- ✓ Olive oil (1 tsp.)
- ✓ Maple syrup (1.5 Tbsp.)

Directions:

1. Take out a wok or your own frying pan and get it all heated up on the stove. Add in the olive oil. When that is warm, add in the triangles of tempeh along with the soy sauce, maple syrup, and liquid smoke.
2. Cook these for a bit, making sure to flip over the tempeh so that it has time to absorb all of the liquid. Sprinkle on the pieces of walnut and then when this is warm, set it to the side for now.
3. Now it is time to add the spices, onions, raisins, syrup, parsley, soy sauce, lemon juice, and carrots into a bowl. Toss well to coat and add the pepper and salt to taste. Serve with the tempeh on top and enjoy.

Nutritional values per serving

Calories 263

Carbs 27g

Fat 13g

Protein 14g

Kidney Bean and Feta Cheese Salad

- ➢ Prep time 8 minutes
- ➢ Serves 2

Ingredients:
- ✓ Spring onions (1)
- ✓ Parsley (.5 c.)
- ✓ Vegan feta cheese (.75 c.)
- ✓ Cucumber (.5)
- ✓ Sweetcorn (.5 can)
- ✓ Kidney beans (1 can)

For the dressing:
- ✓ Salt
- ✓ Pepper
- ✓ Honey (1 tsp.)
- ✓ Dried oregano (.5 tsp.)
- ✓ Cumin (1 tsp.)
- ✓ Mustard (1 tsp.)
- ✓ Olive oil (2 Tbsp.)
- ✓ Juice from half a lime.

Directions:
1. We want to make sure that we start this by rinsing and draining off our kidney beans and the sweetcorn. Then we can finely chop up the cilantro and the parsley ad dice up our cucumber and green onion.
2. You can then add all the ingredients from above into a big salad bowl. Make sure to crumble the feta cheese on top and then mix it all together well.
3. In a second bowl, we need to take all of the ingredients for the dressing and mix them well in their own bowl.
4. Add this to the salad and toss around to coat before serving.

Nutritional values per serving

Calories 540

Carbs 54g

Fat 28g

Protein 23g

Lentil Salad

> ➢ Prep time 30 minutes   ➢ Serves 5

Ingredients:
- ✓ Prepared cilantro (.66 c.)
- ✓ Roma tomatoes (2)
- ✓ Red onion (.5)
- ✓ Black beans (15 oz.)
- ✓ Red bell pepper (1)
- ✓ Brown lentils (1 c.)
- ✓ Optional green onions

For the dressing:
- ✓ Salt (.25 tsp.)
- ✓ Oregano (.5 sp.)
- ✓ Cumin (1 tsp.)
- ✓ Minced garlic clove (2)
- ✓ Dijon mustard (1 tsp.)
- ✓ Olive oil (2 Tbsp.)
- ✓ Juice from one lime

Directions:
1. Start this recipe and follow the instructions on the package in order to cook up the lentils. Make sure that they are a bit firm rather than mushy before draining them out.
2. While your lentils are busy cooking, you can work on the dressing. To do this, take all of the ingredients for the dressing and add to a bowl. Take the time to mix them together well.
3. Chop up the cilantro, tomatoes, pepper, and onion at this time. You can then take the prepared lentils and black beans and all of the chopped vegetables and add to a big bowl.
4. Top it all with the dressing and then serve warm when you are ready.

Nutritional values per serving
Calories 285 - Carbs 41g - Fat 6g - Protein 15g

CHAPTER 9: DINNER RECIPES

Vegan Enchiladas

- ➢ Prep time 50 minutes
- ➢ Serves 6

Ingredients:

For the enchiladas:
- ✓ Nutritional yeast (.33 c.)
- ✓ Hemp hearts (.5 c.)
- ✓ Garbanzo beans (1 can)
- ✓ Black bans (1 can)
- ✓ Red bell pepper (1)
- ✓ Onion (1)
- ✓ Tortillas (6)
- ✓ Salt
- ✓ Smoked paprika (1 tsp.)
- ✓ Cumin (2 tsp.)
- ✓ Tomatoes, Roma (3)

Sauce:
- ✓ Pepper
- ✓ Salt
- ✓ Onion powder (.25 tsp.)
- ✓ Garlic powder (.5 tsp.)
- ✓ Chili powder (.5 tsp.)
- ✓ Cumin (2 tsp.)
- ✓ Olive oil (2 Tbsp.)
- ✓ Flour (.25 c.)
- ✓ Tomato paste (.25 c.)
- ✓ Vegetable broth (3 c.)

Directions:

1. To get started on this one, we are going to make the sauce. To do this, we can take out a bowl and combine the flour, onion powder, chili powder, garlic powder, and cumin in a bowl.
2. When that is done, heat up a bit of oil in a pan and then add in the spice and flour mixture along with the tomato paste. Cook for a minute, making sure to stir the whole time.
3. After a minute, you can add in the broth and bring it to a boil. Reduce the heat and let this simmer for a bit. That will take around eight minutes.
4. Now we can work on the enchiladas of this. You can turn on the oven to reach 350 degrees. While that is heating up, take the time to dice up your onion and bell pepper.
5. In a pan, you can add a bit of oil along with those prepared onions and peppers for a bit.

6. Rinse off the beans and dice the tomatoes as those are cooking. Then add the beans, hemp hearts, yeast, paprika, cumin and tomatoes to the frying pan.
7. Give all of this a good stir around and then heat for a bit before you set it aside for now.
8. Prepare a baking dish and then cover the bottom with just a bit of the sauce, but do not use it all.
9. Fill each of the tortillas with the bean mixture that we have and then roll them up before adding to the baking dish. Cover these with the remainder of the sauce and then add into the oven.
10. After about 25 minutes, these should be done. Take them out of the oven so they can cool down before adding some of your favorite toppings and serving.

Nutritional values per serving:
Calories 526
Carbs 68g
Fat 19g
Protein 22g

Tex-Mex Tofu with Beans

- ➢ Prep time 25 minutes
- ➢ Serves 4

Ingredients:
- ✓ Pepper and salt to taste
- ✓ Chili powder (1 tsp.)
- ✓ Paprika (2 tsp.)
- ✓ Cumin (2 tsp.)
- ✓ Lime juice (1 Tbsp.)
- ✓ Minced garlic clove (1)
- ✓ Pitted avocado (1)
- ✓ Diced onion, purple (1)
- ✓ Olive oil (2 Tbsp.)
- ✓ Firm tofu (14 oz.)
- ✓ Brown rice, dry (1 c.)
- ✓ Black beans, dry (1 c.)

Directions:
1. Take some time to prepare the black beans and the brown rice by following the directions on the package.
2. While those are getting ready, we can slice up the tofu into cubes. Then heat up a bit of oil in a skillet. Add in the onions and then cook to make them nice and soft.
3. After 5 minutes of cooking the onion, you can add in the tofu and cook for a few more minutes, flipping around the cubes on a regular basis.
4. In the meantime, slice the avocado up and then leave on the side for now. Lower the heat a bit and mix in the cumin, garlic, and the prepared black beans.
5. Make sure to stir all of this so that it can be combined and then heat all the way through.
6. After 5 minutes, you can add in the rest of the lime juice and spices. Mix it all the way through and remove the skillet from the heat.
7. Serve this tofu and beans with some of the rice and then garnish with some of the avocados as well.

Nutritional values per serving
Calories 315 - Carbs 28g - Fat 17g - Protein 12.7g

Tofu Cacciatore

- ➤ Prep time 45 minutes
- ➤ Serves 3

Ingredients:
- ✓ Drained tofu (14 oz.)
- ✓ Olive oil (1 Tbsp.)
- ✓ Carrots, matchstick (1 c.)
- ✓ Diced onion, sweet (1)
- ✓ Diced green bell pepper (1)
- ✓ Diced tomatoes (28 oz.)
- ✓ Tomato paste (4 oz.)
- ✓ Balsamic vinegar (.5 Tbsp.)
- ✓ Soy sauce (1 Tbsp.)
- ✓ Maple syrup (1 Tbsp.)
- ✓ Garlic powder (1 Tbsp.)
- ✓ Italian seasoning (1 Tbsp.)
- ✓ Pepper and salt to your taste

Directions:
1. Take the tofu and chop it into the cubes in the size that you would like. Now we can bring out a skillet and heat up some of the oil inside until nice and hot.
2. When that happens, it is time to add the bell peppers, carrots, garlic, and onions. Let these all cook together until they turn translucent.
3. After ten minutes, making sure you stir often to prevent any burning, the mixture is done.
4. When this part is done, combine the Italian seasoning, garlic powder, maple syrup, soy sauce and balsamic vinegar inside of the pan.
5. You want to stir this while adding in the diced tomatoes and the tomato paste. Mix in all of the ingredients until they are combined and then add in the tofu.
6. This is when we need to cover up the pot and turn down the heat just a bit. Allow the mixture some time to simmer so the sauce has some time to thicken.
7. After 20 minutes of this cooking, you can serve this in a bowl with some pepper and salt and then enjoy it.

Nutritional values per serving

Calories 274 - Carbs 34g - Fat 9.5g - Protein 13g

Mushroom Stroganoff

- ➢ Prep time 30 minutes
- ➢ Servs 4

Ingredients:

- ✓ Noodles (2 c.)
- ✓ Chopped onion (1)
- ✓ Vegetable broth (2 c.)
- ✓ Almond flour (2 Tbsp.)
- ✓ Tamari (1 Tbsp.)
- ✓ Tomato paste (1 tsp.)
- ✓ Lemon juice (1 tsp.)
- ✓ Chopped mushrooms (3 c.)
- ✓ Thyme (1 tsp.)
- ✓ Raw spinach (3 c.)
- ✓ Apple cider vinegar (1 Tbsp.)
- ✓ Olive oil (1 Tbsp.)
- ✓ Pepper and salt to your tasting
- ✓ Diced parsley (2 Tbsp.)

Directions:

1. Take some time to prepare the noodles by following the instructions on the package.
2. While that is cooking, heat up a bit of olive oil in a skillet until it is nice and warm. When that happens, you can add in the chopped onion and let it cook until soft.
3. After five minutes of cooking the onion, stir in the lemon juice, tomato paste, tamari, vegetable broth, and the flour and cook to heat all the way through.
4. After that three minutes are done, add in the salt, thyme, and mushrooms and cover up the skillet to cook. We want to cook this until we get mushrooms that are nice and tender.
5. When seven more minutes have gone by, we can turn down the heat a bit and add in the vinegar, spinach, and cooked noodles. Season a bit with some pepper and salt.
6. Cover up that skillet a second time and cook a bit longer, another 10 minutes, so that the flavors are able to combine.
7. Serve this right away.

Nutritional values

Calories 200 - Carbs 28g - Fat 6.5g - Protein 8g

BBQ Grits and Greens

> ➢ Prep time 60 minutes
> ➢ Serves 4

Ingredients:
- ✓ Salt (1 tsp.)
- ✓ Garlic cloves (2)
- ✓ Olive oil (2 Tbsp.)
- ✓ Diced white onion (.25 c.)
- ✓ Grits (1 c.)
- ✓ BBQ sauce (.5 c.)
- ✓ Chopped collard greens (3 c.)
- ✓ Vegetable broth (3 c.)
- ✓ Tempeh (14 oz.)

Directions:
1. To start this recipe, take the time to heat up the oven to 400 degrees. While that is warming up, take out the tempeh and slice it up thinly before adding with the BBQ sauce into a baking dish.
2. Set this aside and give it some time to marinate for as long as needed.
3. Take out a frying pan and heat up just one tablespoon of the oil inside of it. When that is warm, add in the garlic and cook to make nice and fragrant. Add the collard greens and cook until these are dark and wilted.
4. Take your pan off the heat and then cover the BBQ sauce and tempeh with some foil. Place this whole baking dish into the oven and let it bake for a bit.
5. After 15 minutes of baking, we can uncover that pan and let it bake a bit longer, allowing the tempeh to get crispy and brown.
6. After that ten minutes, we can take this out of the oven and set it to the side.
7. While the tempeh is cooking, heat up the rest of the oil in the frying pan and cook the onion until they are brown. Add in the vegetable broth and bring it all to a boil before turning down to low.
8. Whisk in your grits to this simmering broth. Add the rest of the salt and then put the lid on top to cook.
9. Let these ingredients all simmer together for a bit so the grits have time to get creamy and soft. Serve the collard greens and tempeh on the grits and enjoy.

Nutritional values

Calories 394 - Carbs 39g - Fat 17.6g - Protein 20g

Easy Burritos

- ➢ Prep time 50 minutes
- ➢ Serves 4

Ingredients:

- ✓ Salt (.5 tsp.)
- ✓ Cilantro (1 Tbsp.)
- ✓ Salsa (.75 c.)
- ✓ Diced avocado (1)
- ✓ Tortilla wraps (4)
- ✓ Potatoes (2)
- ✓ Portobello mushrooms (3)

For the marinade:

- ✓ Teriyaki sauce (.25 c.)
- ✓ Minced garlic (1 Tbsp.)
- ✓ Lime juice (1 Tbsp.)
- ✓ Water (.33 c.)

Directions:

1. Turn on the oven to start this and heat it up to 400 degrees. While the oven is getting nice and warm, you can add some oil onto a sheet pan and then set it to the side.
2. Bring out a bowl and combine together the garlic, teriyaki, lime juice, and water.
3. Slice up the mushrooms so that they are nice and thin and then add these into the other marinade. Allow this to sit for a maximum o three hours.
4. Now it is time to slice up the potatoes to look kind of like French fries. Sprinkle the fries with some salt and then move them over to the prepared sheet pan.
5. Place these fries into the oven and let them bake to become crispy. After half an hour, you can take these out and set to the side.
6. Bring out a frying pan now and heat it up with the mushroom slices and the rest of the marinade liquid as well. cook these until all of the liquid is gone and evaporated.
7. After ten minutes or so, take these off the heat. Start to assemble the tortillas by adding in a big scoop of the mushrooms and a handful of the potato sticks.
8. Top it all with the cilantro, sliced avocados, and salsa before enjoying it.

Nutritional values per serving

Calories 239 - Carbs 34g - Fat 9g - Protein 5g

Fajitas

- ➤ Prep time 30 minutes
- ➤ Serves 8

Ingredients:
- ✓ Salt
- ✓ Cayenne pepper (.25 tsp.)
- ✓ Garlic powder (1 tsp.)
- ✓ Chili powder (1 tsp.)
- ✓ Lime juice (1 tsp.)
- ✓ Tortilla wraps (6)
- ✓ Olive oil (2 Tbsp.)
- ✓ Sliced portobello mushrooms (3)
- ✓ Chopped onion, sweet (1)
- ✓ Mashed avocado (1)
- ✓ Sliced poblano pepper (1)
- ✓ Diced bell pepper, green (1)
- ✓ Black beans, dry (1 c.)

Directions:
1. Take some time to prepare the black beans using the method that you prefer.
2. When this is done, we can heat up the oil inside one of our frying pans until it is hot. Then add in the bell peppers and the poblano peppers along with half the onion. Add a bit of salt to your own tastes.
3. Cook these vegetables so they have time to get browned and are tender. After ten minutes it is time to add in the black beans and cook until all warmed out.
4. This is the time that we need to add in the mushrooms to the skillet and turn down the heat to a low setting. Stir around the ingredients and cook until the mushrooms are about half their size. Then take it off the heat when this is done.
5. Take out a bowl and combine the rest of the onions with the avocado and the rest of the oil. Mix in some lime juice and add some of the other seasonings as needed.
6. Spread the guacamole that we have onto the tortilla and then add in a big spoon of the prepared mushroom mixture. Serve this and enjoy it right away.

Nutritional values per serving
Calories 264 - Carbs 28g - Fat 14g -Protein 6.8g

Farro Protein Bowls

- ➢ Prep time 40 minutes
- ➢ Serves 2

Ingredients:
- ✓ Lemon wedges (4)
- ✓ Roasted almonds (2 Tbsp.)
- ✓ Hummus (.25 c.)
- ✓ Mixed greens (2 c.)
- ✓ Pepper
- ✓ Salt
- ✓ Uncooked farro (.5 c.)
- ✓ Diced sweet potatoes (1 c.)
- ✓ Diced carrots (1 c.)
- ✓ Organic cooking oil (2 tsp.)
- ✓ Prepared chickpeas (15 oz.)
- ✓ Smoky tempeh strips (4 oz.)
- ✓ Water (1.25 c.)

Directions:
1. To start this recipe, we can turn on the oven and let it heat up to 350 degrees. While that is heating up, add the sweet potatoes to a bowl with the carrots, a small bit of oil and the pepper and salt and mix around to coat.
2. Move this prepared mixture to a baking tray, but only have it take up about a third of the tray.
3. Then it is time to work on the chickpeas. Add these to a bowl with a bit of the oil and some salt and pepper to coat. Toss around to combine and then add onto the baking tray as well.
4. You will want to finish up the room on the baking tray with some of the tempeh strips. When all of these are set up, add the sheet to the oven to roast.
5. After half an hour, you can take these out and give them time to cool down. Make sure to flip them around about halfway through the process.
6. While the stuff is cooking in the oven, you can take out a small pan and add the grains of farro, water, and some salt there. Turn it up to a boil, and then reduce to a simmer until it all is soft.
7. After 25 minutes, this will be done and you can divide the farro between two bowls. Remove the tray from the oven at this time and divide it up as well.
8. Top all of this with the almonds, hummus, and lemon wedges.

Nutritional values per serving
Calories 485 - Carbs 73g - Fat 15g - Protein 25g

Seitan Wings

- ➢ Prep time 30 minutes
- ➢ Serves 4 (each serving has four wings in it)

Ingredients:

For the sauce:

- ✓ ketchup (1 Tbsp.)
- ✓ Lime juice (1 Tbsp.)
- ✓ Vegan butter (.5 c.)
- ✓ Hot sauce (.5 c.)

Breading:

- ✓ Panko breadcrumbs (.5 c.)
- ✓ Flour (.5 c.)
- ✓ Paprika (.5 Tbsp.)
- ✓ Salt
- ✓ Oil (2 Tbsp.)
- ✓ Soy milk (1 c.)
- ✓ Lime juice (1 Tbsp.)

For the seitan:

- ✓ Sliced mushrooms (1 c.)
- ✓ Chopped onions (.33 c.)
- ✓ Minced garlic (1 Tbsp.)
- ✓ Olive oil (2 Tbsp.)
- ✓ Ground sage (2 tsp.)
- ✓ Ground thyme (1.5 tsp.)
- ✓ Ground marjoram (1 tsp.)
- ✓ Ground rosemary (.75 tsp.)
- ✓ Nutmeg (.5 tsp.)
- ✓ Pepper (.5 tsp.)
- ✓ Salt (1 tsp.)
- ✓ Vegetable broth (.5 c.)
- ✓ Vital wheat gluten (1 c.)

Directions:

1. To start this recipe, we need to take the time to heat the oven to 400 degrees. Then we can add the onion, garlic, and mushrooms to a blender to pulse.

2. Add in the oil, salt, and the rest of the spices that are in the section above for the seitan and pulse it a few more times.

3. Add in the broth here and pulse a bit longer to make a nice smooth paste. Then add in the gluten and process to make the whole thing into a kind of dough.

4. Roll out this dough so that it is able to turn into pieces that are shaped like fingers and then flatten them each out.

5. Then it is time for us to work on making the breading. To do this, we just need to take out a bowl and mix together the pepper, salt, paprika, flour, and breadcrumbs together.

6. In a new bowl, mix the lime juice and the soy milk to make our binding for the brad.

7. Dip all of the pieces of seitan into the lime and soy mixture, and then dump into the breadcrumb mixture before adding to the baking tray. Add to the oven when all of the pieces are done.

8. After 20 minutes of cooking, we can take these out to cool down. The last thing to work on is the sauce. To make this, take out a pan and add the hot sauce, ketchup, lime juice, and butter and heat it up.

9. After 5 minutes, you can pour into a little serving bowl and serve the wings inside.

Nutritional values per serving:
Calories 572 - Carbs 36g - Fat 32g - Protein 28g

Easy Dinner Tacos

> ➤ Prep time 40 minutes
> ➤ Serves 3

Ingredients:
- ✓ Coconut oil (1 Tbsp.)
- ✓ Organic tempeh (8 oz.)
- ✓ Taco shells (6)

For the marinade:
- ✓ Onion powder (.25 tsp.)
- ✓ Garlic powder (.5 tsp.)
- ✓ Tamari (1 Tbsp.)
- ✓ Veggie broth (3 Tbsp.)

For the teriyaki sauce:
- ✓ Liquid smoke (.25 tsp.)
- ✓ Corn starch (.5 tsp.)
- ✓ Garlic powder (.5 tsp.)
- ✓ Apple cider vinegar (1 tsp.)
- ✓ Sriracha (1 tsp.)
- ✓ Maple syrup (2 Tbsp.)
- ✓ Olive oil (1 tsp.)
- ✓ Tamari (4 Tbsp)

For the Asian slaw:
- ✓ Pepper (.25 tsp.)
- ✓ Salt (.25 tsp.)
- ✓ Sriracha (1 Tbsp.)
- ✓ Dijon mustard (1 Tbsp.)
- ✓ Maple syrup (1 Tbsp.)
- ✓ Tamari (.5 Tbs.)
- ✓ Lime juice (1 Tbsp.)
- ✓ Sesame oil (2 Tbs.)
- ✓ Apple cider vinegar (.25 c.)
- ✓ Chopped scallions (3)
- ✓ Grated carrots (1 c.)
- ✓ Shredded red cabbage (1 c.)
- ✓ Shredded green cabbage (1 c.)

Directions:

1. To start this recipe, we are going to work on the slaw. Just take out a bowl, put all of the ingredients inside, and then mix it up well.
2. To make the marinade, we just need to find a second bowl, add in all of the ingredients for that part, and mix well. Set to the side for now.
3. The third thing that we need to do here is to work on our teriyaki sauce. To do this, just add the ingredients inside a bowl and then mix it around.
4. Now it is time to work on the tempeh. We can d this by slicing into triangles. Add these to the marinade that we just made and then set to the side for a bit.
5. After 20 minutes, this should be ready. You can take out a skillet and heat it up. Add the tempeh into it and cook for a few minutes on each side to make nice and crispy.
6. Take the tempeh out of the heat, and then dunk it into the teriyaki sauce that we made before. Then add back to the pan to caramelize the tempeh for another half a minute on each side.
7. Take these off the heat and add more of the sauce if you would like. Add to the tacos and serve with the Asian slaw that we made.

Nutritional values per serving:

Calories 550 - Carbs 44g - Fat 31g - Protein 22g

Grilled Tofu Steaks

> ➢ Prep time 25 minutes
> ➢ Serves 2

Ingredients:
- ✓ Soy sauce (2 Tbsp.)
- ✓ Tofu (1 block)
- ✓ Breadcrumbs (.5 c.)
- ✓ Maple syrup (1 tsp.)
- ✓ Sesame oil (2 tsp.)miso paste (2 tsp.)
- ✓ Tomato paste (2 tsp.)

Directions:
1. Take the time to drain off and press the tofu. Your goal is to get rid of as much of the water from it as you can. When that is done, you can cut this into four layers to make the strips.
2. In a small bowl, take the time to mix together the sesame oil, syrup, tomato paste, miso paste, and soy sauce.
3. Add some oil to a grilling tray. While that heats up, you can dip the strips of tofu into the sauce before adding them into the breadcrumbs as well. add these onto the tray when that is all done with as well.
4. Add these to the grill and do about ten minutes of grilling on one side and about 6 minutes on another side to make them nice and browned all over. Serve with a salad to enjoy.

Nutritional values per serving:
Calories 357 - Carbs 29g - Fats 14g - Protein 23g

Vegan Hot Dogs

- ➢ Prep time 15 minutes
- ➢ Serves 2 (1 serving is 2 hot dogs)

Ingredients:

- ✓ Condiments and sauces of your choice
- ✓ Chopped onion (.5)
- ✓ Hot dogs or sausages that are vegan (4)
- ✓ Hot dog rolls (4)

Directions:

1. First, we want to turn on the oven and let it heat up to 360 degrees. Then add the vegan hot dogs inside to cook.
2. After 15 minutes, the hot dogs are done and you can take them out of the oven and add to some hot dog rolls.
3. As the sausage is cooking, you can fry up the onions with a bit of oil on high heat. It will take three minutes to soften them up the way that we want, but you can cook a bit longer if you want.
4. Spoon these on top of your hot dogs and then finish off with some of the condiments and sauces that you would like.

Nutritional values per serving

Calories 550
Carbs 62g
Fats 19g
Protein 24g

Sausage and Tomato Pasta

- ➢ Prep time 20 minutes
- ➢ Serves 2

Ingredients:

- ✓ Mushrooms (3)
- ✓ Pepper (1)
- ✓ Pasta of choice (2 c.)
- ✓ Vegan sausages (6)

For the tomato sauce:

- ✓ Pepper
- ✓ Salt
- ✓ Chili flakes (1 tsp.)
- ✓ Basil (1 tsp.)
- ✓ Tomato puree (1 Tbsp.)
- ✓ Chopped tomato (1)

Directions:

1. Turn on the oven and give it some time to heat up to 260 degrees. Then add the sausages inside and let them cook up. Look at the instructions on the package to see how long they go.
2. Then bring out a pot and add some water to it. Bring this to a boil and then cook up the pasta until it is all done.
3. Then we need a frying pan and we can add up a few tablespoons of oil inside. As this is heating up, you can chop the mushrooms and peppers and then add them to the pan to cook.
4. After five minutes there will be done. Then as these are cooking, you can add all of the ingredients for the sauce into the blender and pulse to make smooth, but not super thin in the process.
5. Add your sauce to the same pan as the vegetables and let it simmer, not getting too hot, for a bit.
6. When the pasta is all done, you can take the pot off the heat and then drain it all out. Add it back to the pan and then top with the sauce and vegetable mix.
7. Take the vegan sausages out of the oven and slice up. Add to the pasta and mix around before serving.

Nutritional values per serving

Calories 426 - Carbs 54g - Protein 32g - Fats 9g

Mongolian Seitan

> ➢ Prep time 30 minutes
> ➢ Serves 6

Ingredients:

For the sauce:
- ✓ Coldwater (2 Tbsp.)
- ✓ Cornstarch (2 tsp.)
- ✓ Coconut or brown sugar (.5 c. and 2 Tbsp.)
- ✓ Soy sauce (.5 c.)
- ✓ Red pepper flakes (.33 tsp.)
- ✓ Chinese five-spice (.33 tsp.)
- ✓ Grated garlic (3 cloves)grated ginger (.5 tsp.)
- ✓ Vegetable oil (2 tsp.)

For the prepared seitan:
- ✓ Seitan cubed (1 lb.)
- ✓ Vegetable oil (1.5 Tbsp.)

For serving:
- ✓ Sliced scallions
- ✓ Toasted sesame seeds

Directions:

1. Start by heating up the oil on medium heat in your pan. When that is warm, you can add in the ginger and the garlic and stir around.
2. About half a minute later, it is time to add in the red pepper flakes and five spices and cook until fragrant as well.
3. Now it is time to add in the sugar and soy sauce and then lower the heat so these ingredients will simmer. Go until the sugar is dissolved.
4. After 5 minutes, whisk together the water and the cornstarch in a small bowl and then add to the pan to cook until the sauce starts to look a bit glossy.
5. Get the heat down to the lowest setting possible and let it simmer nice and slowly until it is time to add in the seitan.
6. To make our seitan, we want to bring out another pan or a skillet and heat up the vegetables. Add in the seitan and cook for a bit so that it gets browned and starts to be crisp around the edges.
7. This is the time where we reduce the heat to low and add some of the sauce to the pan. Make sure to stir around so that the seitan pieces will get nice and coated.
8. When that is done, you can take it off the heat and serve hot with the vegetables of your choice or with some rice.

Nutritional values per serving

Calories 272 - Carbs 22g - Fats 10g - Protein 25g

Vegan Burgers

- ➢ Prep time 15 minutes
- ➢ Serves 2 (1 serving is 2 burgers)

Ingredients:
- ✓ Ketchup or relish to your taste
- ✓ Sliced tomato (.5)
- ✓ Pulled lettuce leaves (.25)
- ✓ Vegan burgers of choice (4)
- ✓ Burger buns (4)

Directions:
1. Take the burgers out of their package and heat up the oven so that it reaches 360 degrees. Add the burgers inside and let them cook for a bit.
2. After 20 minutes, the burgers will b done and you can take them out of the oven to cool down.
3. While that happens, you can slice up your tomato and then pull the leaves off the lettuce that you want to use.
4. Add the prepared burgers onto some buns and top with the tomato and lettuce. Add on any of the sauces that you would like to use as well here.

Nutritional values
Calories 700 - Carbs 65g - Fats 27g - Protein 44g

Lentil Loaf with BBQ

- ➢ Prep time 90 minutes
- ➢ Serves 2 (2 serving is four slices)

Ingredients:
For the loaf:
- ✓ Corn (.5 c.)
- ✓ Chipotle chili spice (.5 tsp.)
- ✓ Ground flaxseed (3 Tbsp.)
- ✓ Grind coarse cornmeal (.5 c.)
- ✓ BBQ (1 c.)
- ✓ Water (.25 c.)
- ✓ Salt (.25 tsp.)
- ✓ Minced garlic (1 Tbsp.)
- ✓ Chopped white onion (.5 c.)
- ✓ Salt (.5 tsp.)
- ✓ Lentils (1 c.)

For the BBQ:
- ✓ Liquid smoke (2 tsp.)
- ✓ Regular molasses (2 Tbsp.)
- ✓ Dark balsamic vinegar (2 Tbsp.)
- ✓ Maple syrup (2 Tbsp.)
- ✓ Mustard (1 Tbsp. and 1 tsp.)
- ✓ Chili powder (1 tsp. and 1 Tbsp.)
- ✓ Garlic powder (.5 Tbsp.)
- ✓ Salt (.25 tsp.)
- ✓ Water (.5 c.)
- ✓ Tomato paste (.5 c.)

Directions:
1. We want to start this one out by making the sauce. All that is needed for this one is to take all of the ingredients and add them to a bowl, mixing around well.
2. Take out a pan and add in just a bit of oil. When that is hot, add in the garlic and the onions and let them cook until soft.

3. Take out your blender here and puree half of the lentils inside. Then add the garlic and onion to the lentils while mixing in .75 cup of the BBQ sauce here.
4. We also want to add in the flaxseed, cornmeal, and chipotle spice here. Give it all a nice stir until it is thick and sticky before adding in the corn.
5. This is the time to add some baking paper to a metal loaf. Leave a bit over the edges so that it is easier to pull out later.
6. Pour your mixture into the prepared pan and then set it to the side for about twenty minutes or so. At that time, let the oven heat up to 360 degrees for a bit.
7. When you are ready, you can spread the rest of the sauce over your loaf and then add it to the oven. We want to cook until this is nice and firm.
8. After an hour of cooking, take the loaf out of the oven and give it some time to cool down. Then you can take it out of the tin and slice up before serving.

Nutritional values
Calories 520
Carbs 120g
Fats 7g
Protein 23g

Lentil Ragu

- ➢ Prep time 50 minutes
- ➢ Serves 4

Ingredients:

- ✓ Courgettes sliced into noodles (2)
- ✓ Balsamic vinegar (2 Tbsp.)
- ✓ Dried oregano (1 tsp.)
- ✓ Vegetable bouillon (1 liter)
- ✓ Passata (1 package)dried red lentils (500 grams)
- ✓ Quartered button mushrooms (.5 c.)
- ✓ Chopped onion (2)
- ✓ Chopped garlic cloves (40chopped carrots (2)
- ✓ Chopped celery sticks (3)
- ✓ Rapeseed oil (2 Tbsp.)

Directions:

1. Take out a pan and heat up two tablespoons of the oil. When this is nice and warm, add the onions, garlic, celery, and carrots inside.
2. Fry these for about 5 minutes on high heat until they start to get soft. Then add in the mushrooms and fry a bit longer.
3. After two minutes of those frying, it is time to add in the balsamic vinegar, oregano, passata, bouillon, and lentils.
4. Cover up the pan here and let it simmer until the lentils are nice and tender, which can take around half an hour. Check on it occasionally to stir and make sure that nothing is sticking. If you need to, add just a bit of water to the mixture.
5. Then we can heat up the rest of the oil in another pan and add in the sliced up courgette. Fry this to make it warm and soft.
6. Serve the Ragu that we made with the courgette and enjoy it.

Nutritional values per serving

Calories 578 - Carbs 87g - Fat 7g - Protein 18g

Seitan and Black Bean Stir Fry

> ➢ Prep time 15 minutes
> ➢ Serves 2

Ingredients:

For the sauce:
- ✓ Chinese five-spice powder (1 tsp.)
- ✓ Soy sauce (2 Tbsp.)
- ✓ Garlic cloves (3)
- ✓ Brown sugar (75g)
- ✓ Black beans (400g)
- ✓ Chopped red chili (1)
- ✓ Peanut butter (1 Tbsp.)
- ✓ Rice vinegar (2 Tbsp.)

For the stir fry:
- ✓ Cooked noodles or rice
- ✓ Sliced spring onions (2)
- ✓ Chopped pak choi (300 grams)
- ✓ Sliced red pepper (1)
- ✓ Vegetable oil (3 Tbsp.)
- ✓ Corn flour (1 Tbsp.)
- ✓ Marinated seitan pieces (350 grams)

Directions:

1. Take some time to cook up the rice or the rice noodles that you want to use. You can just follow the instructions on the package to get this one done.
2. While the noodles or rice are cooking, you can work on the sauce. You can add half the black beans with the rest of the sauce ingredients into a blender.
3. Blend these together until they are smooth. Add into a pan and cook up for about five minutes inside.
4. As the sauce is getting nice and warm, you can add the seitan with the cornflour. Take out a big frying pan and add in a bit of oil. Then add in the seitan and let it cook until it is golden brown in color.
5. After 5 minutes, you can take the seitan off the heat. Add the spring onion, pak choi, and peppers to the pan with a bit of the oil and fry for a few more minutes before adding the seitan back in.
6. Stir it all together for a minute and then serve warm.

Nutritional values per serving

Calories 660

Carbs 74g

Fat 16 g

Protein 44g

Vegan Sausage Rolls

- ➢ Prep time 1 hour
- ➢ Serves 5

Ingredients:
- ✓ Chopped chestnuts (30 gramso)
- ✓ Dijon mustard (2 tsp.)
- ✓ Brown rice miso (1 Tbsp.)
- ✓ Chopped sage leaves (1 Tbsp.)
- ✓ Chopped leeks (2)
- ✓ Olive oil (3 Tbsp.)
- ✓ Chestnut mushrooms (250 grams)
- ✓ Dairy-free milk of choice to glaze
- ✓ Plain flour to use for dusting
- ✓ Pastry puff sheet (1)
- ✓ White breadcrumbs (70 grams)

Directions:
1. You can start this recipe by adding the mushrooms into a blender and then pulse the ingredients until they are chopped up well.
2. Then we can heat up about half of our oil into a frying pan and when it is warm, add the leeks to cook to make them golden brown and soft.
3. After 15 minutes, these leeks should be done and you can take them off the heat and set to the side.
4. Add in the remainder of your oil to the pan and fry up the mushrooms that you blended. This will take about 10 minutes and then you can add in the miso, mustard, sage, and garlic, frying a bit longer.
5. Turn on the oven here and heat it up to 400 degrees. As the oven is heating up, add the mushroom mixture and the leeks into a bowl together along with the breadcrumbs and the chestnuts.
6. Make sure to season this well and mix it to get it into a stuffing mixture. Then roll out the pastry on a surface that has been floured and then arrange this mixture right in the middle of the pastry for now.
7. When that is done, you can roll up the pastry so that it goes around the filling, sealing it up at the seam with the help of a fork. Cut into 10 rolls and add to a prepared baking tray.
8. Brush each piece of this with some milk and then add to the oven to bake. After 25 minutes, they should be a deep golden brown color and you can take them out.
9. Sprinkle on a few sesame seeds before serving.

Nutritional values per serving
Calories 652 - Carbs 54g -Fat 40g - Protein 14g

Spicy Rice in One Pan

> - Prep time 20 minutes
> - Serves 4

Ingredients:
- Spinach (175 grams)
- Handful of raisins
- Chickpeas (400 grams)
- Vegetable stock (450 ml)
- Rinsed basmati rice (250 grams)
- Curry paste (2 Tbsp.)
- Crushed garlic cloves (2)
- Sunflower oil (1 Tbsp.)
- Serve with natural oil.

Directions:
1. Take out a large pan and heat up a bit of oil inside. When it gets nice and warm, then you can go through and add in the curry paste and garlic and let these heat up.
2. After a minute, you can add in the pepper, salt, chickpeas, raisins, vegetable stock, and rice. Stir these together well.
3. Reduce the heat a bit and then cover up the pan, letting it heat up and get warm and cooked through.
4. After about 15 minutes, all of the liquid should be gone and your rice should be tender. Right at the end of the cooking process, add in the cashew nuts and spinach.
5. Serve when it is all done.

Nutritional values per serving
Calories 380
Carbs 66g
Fat 9g
Protein 12g

Vegan Banh Mi

- ➢ Prep time 15 minutes
- ➢ Serves 4

Ingredients:
- ✓ Coriander (.5 pack)
- ✓ Cooked tempeh (175g)
- ✓ Hummus (100 grams)
- ✓ French baguette (1)
- ✓ Golden caster sugar (1 tsp.)
- ✓ White wine vinegar (3 Tbsp.)
- ✓ Shredded raw veggies (150 grams)
- ✓ Hot sauce for serving
- ✓ Mint (.5 pack)

Directions:
1. Turn on the oven and let it heat up to 350 degrees. As the oven is getting nice and warm, you can add the salt, sugar, and vinegar to a bowl along with the vegetables that you shredded up earlier. Toss it all together and combine it before setting it to the side.
2. Next, we can slice up the baguette into four pieces to use for this. Add these into the oven and let them get toasted in the oven. You only need to leave them there for around five minutes.
3. Take each of these from the oven and then cover with some of the hummus, the prepared tempeh slices, and the vegetables. Add some of your chosen herbs on top as well and then serve.

Nutritional values per serving
Calories 338 - Carbs 40g - Protein 16g - Fats 11g

Curried Tofu Wraps

> ➢ Prep time 35 minutes
> ➢ Serves 4

Ingredients:
- ✓ Quartered limes (2)
- ✓ Chapatis (8)
- ✓ Sliced garlic cloves (2)
- ✓ Sliced onions (2)
- ✓ Oli (2 Tbsp.)
- ✓ Tandoori curry paste (2 Tbsp.)
- ✓ Shredded red cabbage (.5)
- ✓ Dairy-free yogurt (4 Tbsp.)
- ✓ Mint sauce (3 Tbsp.)
- ✓ Tofu cubed (600g)

Directions:
1. To start with this recipe, we want to mix together the yogurt, mint sauce, and cabbage. When this is well combined, we can set it to the side.
2. Toss together the tandoori paste with the tofu. Then add a bit of the oil to a frying pan. Add the tandoori tofu to the pan and let it cook for a bit to get all of the sides nice and golden. Take off the heat when this is done.
3. Then we need to use the same pan and add in the onions and garlic. Let these cook too.
4. After another eight minutes, add the tofu back to this pan and cook to heat back up.
5. You can follow the instructions on the package for warming up the chapatis and then fill these up with some of the tofu and the sauce that we made earlier.
6. Serve with a bit of lime and enjoy.

Nutritional values per serving:
Calories 497 - Carbs 38g - Fat 25g - Protein 27g

Chocolate Chip Muffins

- ➤ Prep time 15 minutes
- ➤ Serves 8

Ingredients:
- ✓ vanilla protein powder (2 scoops)
- ✓ applesauce (1 c.)
- ✓ almond or nut butter (.5 c)
- ✓ almond flour (.5 c.)
- ✓ baking powder (1 tsp.)
- ✓ Chocolate chips (.5 c.)

Directions:
1. Take the time to turn on the oven and heat it up to 350 degrees. Then take the time to prepare some muffin tins.
2. As the oven heats up you can take all of the ingredients from above and add into a big mixing bowl, making sure to stir around and get it well combined.
3. Divide this batter between your muffin tins as well as possible and then put it into the oven. A
4. After 15 minutes, the muffins should be done. Take them out and give them a few minutes to cool down before serving.

Nutritional values per serving
Calories 187 - Carbs 15g - Fat 11g - Protein 7g

Black Bean and Chocolate Pudding

- ➢ Prep time 2 hours
- ➢ Serves 2

Ingredients:
- ✓ Melted coconut oil (1 Tbsp.)
- ✓ Vanilla (1 tsp.)
- ✓ Salt (1 pinch)
- ✓ Medjool dates (2 pitted)
- ✓ Maple syrup (2 Tbsp.)
- ✓ Cocoa powder (.25 c.)
- ✓ Coconut or almond milk (4 Tbsp.)
- ✓ Black beans, cooked (1 c.)

Optional servings:
- ✓ Peanut butter
- ✓ Sliced banana
- ✓ Sliced strawberries
- ✓ Coconut whipped cream

Directions:
1. To start, we want to drain and then rinse the black beans off so they are ready. Then take out the blender and add the beans inside.
2. Add in the rest of the ingredients here and then blitz to make them nice and smooth.
3. You can then pass this new mixture through a fine-mesh strainer so all of the extra pieces are taken out.
4. Scoop this mixture into some serving containers and then add to the fridge so that it can set and get thicker. This will take around two hours or more.
5. Serve chilled with some fruit on top if you would like.

Nutritional values per serving
Calories 463 - Carbs 50g - Fat 29g - Protein 14g

Hazelnut and Chocolate Bars

- ➢ Prep time 15 minutes
- ➢ Serves 4

Ingredients:
- ✓ Brown rice syrup (3 Tbsp.)
- ✓ Cashew butter (.25 c.)
- ✓ Almond milk (.33 c.)
- ✓ Unsweetened cocoa powder (.25 c.)
- ✓ Chopped hazelnuts (.25 c.)
- ✓ Vegan protein powder, chocolate (1 c.)

Directions:
1. To start this recipe, take out a bowl and add in the hazelnuts, cocoa, and protein powder. Mix using your whisk to help combine well.
2. You can then continue on with this by adding in the brown rice syrup, cashew butter, and almond milk. Whisk to make them combined, but realize that it is going to start to turn into a dough and bit a bit sticky.
3. Layout some parchment paper on a tray and then add the dough to the middle. Press it out with a rolling pin or your hands.
4. Put this whole tray into the fridge to set for about four hours. Or if you need this to go faster, add to the freezer and leave it there for an hour and a half.
5. Slice this up into 8 bars and then serve.

Nutritional values per serving
Calories 296 - Carbs 21.3g - Fat 14.2g - Protein 21g

Sweet Lentil Bites

- ➢ Prep time 30 minutes
- ➢ Servs 8

Ingredients:
- ✓ Chopped almonds (.25 c.)
- ✓ Maple syrup (.5 c.)
- ✓ Almond butter (.5 c.)
- ✓ Shredded coconut (.25 c.)
- ✓ Pumpkin seeds (.25 c.)
- ✓ Cooking oats (1.5 c.)
- ✓ Salt
- ✓ Allspice (.5 tsp.)
- ✓ Cinnamon (.5 tsp.)
- ✓ Coconut oil (.5 Tbsp.)
- ✓ Green lentils (.75 c.)

Directions:
1. Go through and prepare the lentils using one of your favorite methods to get it done. Then turn on the oven and let it heat up to 375 degrees. While that warms up you can use some parchment paper to line a baking pan.
2. Take the lentils that you just cooked and add to a bowl with the salt, allspice, cinnamon, and coconut oil. Mix it together well.
3. Pour this to that baking pan you prepared and spread them out before adding to the oven. About halfway through the cooking process, you can stir them around.
4. After 20 minutes, take the lentils out of the oven and give time to cool down.
5. Mix together the crushed almonds, maple syrup, almond butter, shredded coconut, seeds, and oats. Add the lentils into here and mix to combine.
6. Roll these all into some balls with the help of an ice cream scoop and then put them onto a plate. Set them into the fridge to harden for an hour and then serve.

Nutritional values per serving

Calories 264 - Carbs 31g - Fat 12g - Protein 7.4g

No-Bake Treats

> ➢ Prep time 20 minutes - Serves 8

Ingredients:
- ✓ Brown rice syrup (.25 c.)
- ✓ Almond milk (2 Tbsp.)
- ✓ Vegan protein powder (.75 c.)
- ✓ Almond butter (.75 c.)
- ✓ Puffy rice cereal (4 c.)
- ✓ Vanilla (1 Tbsp.)
- ✓ Crushed almonds (.33 c.)
- ✓ Shredded coconut (.33 c.)
- ✓ Crushed hazelnuts (.33 c.)
- ✓ Salt (.25 tsp.)

Directions:
1. Take out a nice baking dish that is square and add a bit of paper for baking inside. Set to the side for now.
2. Now we need to work with a pan, and we can heat it up on the stove. When it is set, you can add in the salt, almond butter, protein powder, almond milk, and brown rice syrup.
3. Let these simmer on a low setting until the ingredients start to bubble. Then add in the rice cereal and the vanilla, mixing these together until they are coated well.
4. Move this whole thing into that baking dish that you already prepared and then press down until it is an even thickness all around.
5. Sprinkle the top of this with some coconut and almonds and add to the freezer to let it firm. After an hour, you can take these out and slice into 8 pieces before serving.

Nutritional values per serving:
Calories 191 - Carbs 13g - Fat 11g - Protein 9g

Zucchini Muffins

- ➤ Prep time 40 minutes
- ➤ Serves 8

Ingredients:

- ✓ Quinoa, dry (.5 c.)
- ✓ Coconut oil (2 Tbsp.)
- ✓ Almond flour (1.5 c.)
- ✓ Chopped walnuts (.5 c.)
- ✓ Bananas (2)
- ✓ Applesauce (.5 c.)
- ✓ Maple syrup (.25 c.)
- ✓ Shredded zucchini (.5 c.)
- ✓ Vegan protein powder (1 c.)
- ✓ Dark chocolate chips, vegan (.5 c.)
- ✓ Almond milk (5 Tbsp.)
- ✓ Baking powder (2 tsp.)
- ✓ Cinnamon (.5 tsp.)
- ✓ Vanilla (.5 tsp.)
- ✓ Nutmeg (.5 tsp.)
- ✓ Water (.5 c)

Directions:

1. Go through and prepare the quinoa using the instructions that are on the package. You can also turn on the oven to 400 degrees and then line a muffin pan and get that set up well too.
2. Take out a big bowl and mix together your baking powder, quinoa, walnuts cinnamon, salts, and nutmeg.
3. Take out another bowl that you can use and add the banans and mash it with a fork with the applesauce as well. then stir in the almond milk, protein powder, maple syrup, and protein powder.
4. Combine these two mixtures that we have been working with until they are nice and smooth and there are no lumps in it.
5. Carefully add in the chocolate chips now, as well as the zucchini that you shredded up. Add into the muffin cups, filling them about half the way up.
6. Add to the oven and let it bake for a bit. After 20 minutes, these muffins should be done. You can take them out of the oven and then let them cool down before serving.

Nutritional values per serving

Calories 354 - Carbs 30g - Fat 19g - Protein 14g

Lemon Bars

- ➢ Prep time 10 minutes
- ➢ Serves 6

Ingredients:
- ✓ Chia seeds (.25 c.)
- ✓ Pecan pieces (.25 c.)
- ✓ Raw cashews (.33 c.)
- ✓ Sunflower seeds (.33 c.)
- ✓ Pitted dates (2 c.)
- ✓ Vanilla protein powder, vegan (.5 c.)
- ✓ Organic lemon juice (2 Tbsp.)
- ✓ Salt (.25 tsp.)

Directions:
1. Take out the chia seeds and soak them in some water for at least half an hour. When this is done, we can take the time to drain out any water that is left.
2. Then it is time to add the cashews, pecans, chia seeds, and the sunflower seeds into your own food processor. Make sure to pulse and mix these ingredients together until they make a mixture that is crumbly.
3. Add in the juice along with the salt and the dates. Continue to pulse all of these together while you add in your protein powder. We want the mixture to get chunky but still feel like dough.
4. When that happens, we can line a baking sheet with a bit of paper and then move the dough over to it. Use a rolling pin or your own fingers to press this out to make a thick square.
5. Add this whole pan to the freezer and let it stay there for at least 60 minutes, or until the chunk is nice and solid.
6. Take out of the freezer and slice into 8 bars before serving.

Nutritional values per serving:
Calories 272 - Carbs 35g - Fat 11g - Protein 9g

Sunflower Protein Bars

- ➤ Prep time 15 minutes
- ➤ Serves 6

Ingredients:
- ✓ Salt (.25 tsp.)
- ✓ Nutmeg (.25 tsp.)
- ✓ Cinnamon (1 tsp.)
- ✓ Old fashioned oats (1 c.)
- ✓ Puffy rice cereal (1 c.)
- ✓ Chocolate vegan protein powder (1 c.)
- ✓ Vanilla (2 tsp.)
- ✓ Maple syrup (.5 c.)
- ✓ Sunflower butter (.5 c.)

Directions:
1. To start this recipe, bring out a bowl and add together the salt, nutmeg, cinnamon, protein powder, rice cereal, and oats. Set this to the side.
2. Take out another bowl that you can use and add in the maple syrup and the sunflower butter. Heat it up in the microwave for half a minute.
3. Take the mixture out of the microwave and mix the heated ingredients with the dry ingredients.
4. Stir this well and then add in the vanilla. Use a whisk to make sure that the lumps are gone and you have a nice and smooth mixture.
5. Spread this into a dish that is shallow and then line with some paper. Pack it down with a spoon to make sure that all of the air bubbles are gone.
6. Move to the freezer and let it sit for a bit. After about 20 minutes, we can take the dish out and slice into six bars before serving.

Nutritional values per serving:
Calories 188 - Carbs 22g - Fat 6.8g - Protein 9.6g

Southwest Stuffed Bowls

- ➢ Prep time 30 minutes
- ➢ Serves 4

Ingredients:
- ✓ Hummus (.25 c.)
- ✓ Dry black beans (1 c.)
- ✓ Dry chickpeas (.25 c.)
- ✓ Water or you can work with vegetable broth (1 c.)
- ✓ Chopped onion, purple (.5)
- ✓ Garlic powder (1 tsp.)
- ✓ Cumin (.5 tsp.)
- ✓ Paprika (.25 tsp.)
- ✓ Avocados halved (4)
- ✓ Salt (1 pinch)
- ✓ Lime juice (1 tsp.)
- ✓ Salsa (.25 c.)

Directions:
1. Take the time to prepare both the chickpeas and the black beans using some of your favorite methods ahead of time.
2. Bring out a pot and heat it up on a higher temperature. Add either the vegetable broth or water. When these are warm, it is time to add in all of the spices, onions, chickpeas, and black beans.
3. When these are in, you can stir to combine all of the ingredients and then cook up the mixture so that most of the liquid is all gone.
4. After 15 minutes, this should be all done. In the meantime, you can sprinkle the halves of avocado with the salt and a bit of lime juice. You can serve these halves with some of the bean mixtures and then top with the salsa and hummus and enjoy.

Nutritional values per serving:
Calories 351 - Carbs 33g - Fat 20g - Protein 10g

Brownie Bars

- ➢ Prep time 15 minutes
- ➢ Serves 3

Ingredients:
- ✓ Chocolate vegan protein powder (2.5 c.)
- ✓ Cocoa powder (.5 c.)
- ✓ Quick style oats (.5 c.)
- ✓ Vanilla (1 tsp.)
- ✓ Nutmeg (.25 tsp.)
- ✓ Agave nectar (2 Tbsp.)
- ✓ Cold coffee that is brewed (1 c.)

Directions:
1. Take out a baking dish that is square and line it with a bit of paper. Set this to the side for now.
2. Bring out a big bowl and then mix the dry ingredients together. When those are done, add in the cold coffee, nectar, and the vanilla, making sure that you stir this around so that the lumps are no longer there.
3. Then it is time to pour this batter into your dish, taking the time to press it down so it gets into the corners well.
4. Add this into the fridge so that it has time to get nice and firm. After four hours, it will be done. You can also add to the freezer to speed things up as this only takes about 60 minutes.
5. When that is done, take the dish out of the fridge and then slice into 6 pieces before serving.

Nutritional values per serving:
Calories 213
Carbs 17g
Fat 4g
Protein 27g

Chewy Butter Balls

- ➢ Prep time 15 minutes
- ➢ Serves 2

Ingredients:
- ✓ Carob chips (1 Tbsp.)
- ✓ Puffy rice cereal (1 c.)
- ✓ Vanilla (1 Tbsp.)
- ✓ Almond butter (.25 c.)
- ✓ Vegan protein powder, vanilla (.5 c.)
- ✓ Maple syrup (2 Tbsp.)

Directions:
1. Bring out a bowl and add inside the vanilla, almond butter, protein powder, and maple syrup. Mix until well combined.
2. Take the bowl and add it to the microwave. Cook and heat up until they are nice and melted.
3. Add in the puffy rice cereal along with the carob chips. Make sure to stir it all together so that it is nice and even one more time.
4. You can then line a sheet pan with a bit of parchment paper and then use a spoon to scoop out the mixture and make it into some small balls in your hands.
5. Press each of these firmly together to help prevent the crumbling and then add back onto the pan. Put into the freezer to set for about an hour. Enjoy when ready.

Nutritional values per serving
Calories 329
Carbs 25g
Fat 16.5g
Protein 21g

Carrot Cake

> ➢ Prep time 10 minutes
> ➢ Serves 4

Ingredients:

For the cake:
- ✓ Vanilla protein powder (3 Tbsp.)
- ✓ Pecans (.5 c.)
- ✓ Raisins (.5 c.)
- ✓ Stevia (1 tsp.)
- ✓ Ground nutmeg (.25 tsp.)
- ✓ Cinnamon (1 tsp.)
- ✓ Orange zest (2 Tbsp.)
- ✓ Orange juice (2 Tbsp.)
- ✓ Ground almonds (.5 c.)
- ✓ Dried coconut (.5 c.)
- ✓ Carrots (2)

For the frosting:
- ✓ Water as needed
- ✓ Maple syrup (2 Tbsp.)
- ✓ Coconut oil (2 Tbsp.)
- ✓ Lemon juice (2 Tbsp.)
- ✓ Soaked cashews (2 c.)

Directions:

1. To start with this recipe, we want to bring out our blender and add in all of the ingredients listed above for the cake inside. Pulse until this is nice and blended and then press the mixture into the pan you are using.
2. Then it is time to make the frosting we want to use. After cleaning out the blender add in all of the ingredients that we listed above for the frosting.
3. Pulse these in the blender until they are well mixed. You can add in some more water if you need to make it a bit smoother.
4. Use this to frost the cake and enjoy it right away.

Nutritional values per serving

Calories 779 - Carbs 45g - Fats 51g - Protein 35g

Protein Oat and Banana Balls

- ➢ Prep time 5 minutes
- ➢ Serves 4

Ingredients:
- ✓ Banana (1)
- ✓ Vegan protein powder, vanilla (1 serving)
- ✓ Rolled oats (85 grams)

Directions:
1. Bring out the blender and add in the protein powder and oats. Blitz these together until the oats are chopped, but you do not want it to be all the way smooth.
2. Add the banana into this and then combine to make a coarse but pliable dough.
3. When this is done, you can roll these into 12 balls and then add to the fridge and enjoy it when ready.

Nutritional values per serving

Calories 141 - Carbs 24g - Fats 7g - Protein 6g

***

Protein Brownies

- ➢ Prep time 20 minutes
- ➢ Serves 9

Ingredients:
- ✓ Vegan protein powder, chocolate (2 scoops)
- ✓ Cocoa powder (.25 c.)
- ✓ Almond butter (.5 c.)
- ✓ Bananas (3)

Directions:
1. Take the time here to turn on the oven and let it heat up to 360 degrees. Then you can take the time to bring out a small cake pan and grease it all up.
2. Bring out a bowl and add in the nut butter. Add to the microwave and let it heat up until nice and smooth.
3. Take out a food processor and blender and add in the nut butter, protein powder, cocoa powder, and banana. Blitz these together until they are nice and smooth.
4. Pour this whole thing into that pan we prepared and add to the oven. Bake until the brownies are nice and firm.
5. After 20 minutes, the brownies should be done. Allow them some time to cool down all the way and then slice up.

Nutritional values

Calories 134 - Carbs 15g - Fats 7g Protein 7g

Oatmeal Raisin Cookies

- ➢ Prep time 30 minutes
- ➢ Serves 5

Ingredients:
- ✓ Vanilla (.5 tsp.)
- ✓ Raisins (1 Tbsp.)
- ✓ Almond milk (.25 c.)
- ✓ Honey (1 Tbsp.)
- ✓ Raw oats (.5 c.)
- ✓ Agave syrup (.25 c.)
- ✓ Protein powder, vanilla (.5 c.)
- ✓ Natural almond butter (3 Tbsp.)

Directions:
1. Add all of your ingredients except for the nuts, chocolate chips, and raisins, into the food processor. Blitz around to make a nice dough that we are able to mold with our hands. Then we can add in the toppings.
2. Divide this into five balls and then add into a baking tray that is lined with some baking paper. Press these down to make some cookies.
3. Turn on the oven and turn it up to 350 degrees. When this is ready, add the cookies inside and let them cook until they are nice and browned on top.
4. After 10 minutes, the cookies should be done. Allow them some time to cool down before you serve.

Nutritional values
Calories 211
Carbs 28g
Fats 7g
Protein 12g

Thank you for making it through to the end of *The Vegan Athlete*. Let's hope it was informative and able to provide you with all of the tools you need to achieve your goals, whatever they may be.

The next step is to start making your own meal plan and figure out what steps you need to follow in order to become a vegan on your own as an athlete. We took the time to talk all about the benefits of this great diet plan, and we even took a look at some of the basic foods that are going to help you get all of your nutrients when you are vegan. There are a lot of misconceptions out there about the vegan diet, but as more and more people learn about how healthy and wholesome it is, and even as more and more bodybuilders and athletes start to try it out and see results as well, it is likely that the rise in popularity will keep ongoing.

In this guidebook, we took the time to go through some of the basics that we need to know when we want to be a vegan athlete. We talked about the vegan before moving on to some of the basics of being an athlete and trying to make this diet plan work. We talked about the importance of protein and how we are able to get enough even on the vegan diet. We looked at some of the unique nutrient requirements of being on the vegan diet when we want to do an anaerobic activity, and how the vegan diet can help. And we even took a look at some of the basics that need to be met if a bodybuilder chooses to be on this kind of diet plan.

We also dived into some of the basics that are necessary for making meals that are vegan and athlete-friendly in the process. This is sometimes the hardest part of the whole thing because we worry about finding meals that are really delicious and good, but then also ones that are going to meet all of our nutrient requirements in the process. This guidebook has a ton of delicious and easy recipes that you are able to use to ensure that both of these requirements are met and you can follow this diet in the manner that you want.

There are so many benefits to going vegan as an athlete and it is so worth your time to learn more get started. This guidebook is going to be the tool that you need to help you there. When you are ready to work with this diet plan to help you get the best performance out of your athletics, make sure to check out this guidebook to help make that dream a reality in no time.

Finally, if you found this book useful in any way, a review on Amazon is always appreciated!